THE
TIE
THAT
BINDS

THE TIE THAT BINDS

Richard B. Wilke

ABINGDON PRESS
NASHVILLE

THE TIE THAT BINDS

Copyright © 2008 by Abingdon Press

This book is printed on acid-free paper.

Library of Congress Cataloging-in-Publication Data
Wilke, Richard B., 1930-
   The tie that binds / Richard Wilke.
      p. cm.
   ISBN 978-0-687-65208-2 (binding: pbk., adhesive perfect : alk. paper)
   1. Church work.   2. Social gospel.   3. Church and social problems.
I. Title.

BV4400.W5155 2008
253—dc22

2007044466

08 09 10 11 12 13 14 15 16 17—10 9 8 7 6 5 4 3 2 1

MANUFACTURED IN THE UNITED STATES OF AMERICA

Contents

Contents

Prologue

Twenty years after I wrote *And Are We Yet Alive?* I thought I would write a sequel and call it *And Are We Still Yet Alive?* It would be an "I told you so," a kick in the pants showing uninterrupted decline in mainline (sideline) churches. Sunday school attendance: down. Membership: down. A handful of new congregational starts in contrast to hundreds of rural and inner-city churches closing their doors.

This plan exploded when my children said, "Don't write about church growth! Nobody cares about that. Write about spiritual matters; lots of others are dealing with organizational renewal."

Then I was run over by a freight train, a crashing avalanche of new experiences. Scores of college kids—Catholics and Baptists, Presbyterians and United Methodists—started raising their hands, clapping, even jumping up and down in chapel. Busloads of church members headed to Mississippi and Louisiana on Katrina mission trips. Pastors began talking about how difficult it is to be in ministry today. Debates over homosexuality threatened to split denominations. DISCIPLE Bible study began going to prison. And the formal, organized church world started falling apart. The headlines highlighted pedophile priests and adulterous pastors. Television featured prominent laypeople who scorched their ledger sheets, politicians who attended church on Sunday and lied on Monday. On one hand, the unchurched are cynical of authority and standoffish from church institutions. Yet on the other hand, spiritual inquiry is sweeping the country.

Some pastors, tired of business as usual, launch out into the deep. Innovative preachers tell their dramatic turnaround congregation stories and encourage others to go and do likewise. Many preachers and church leaders, like me, have visited their churches, studied their books, and tried to learn. Some of our more enterprising pastors have flown halfway across the country to explore ideas from non-United Methodist churches.

But the bad news is, the decline continues unabated.

Reasons abound. This book will explore our weaknesses and give hints for new directions. Under the rubric of connectedness, we will explore where we are disconnected and how we could connect once again. We will observe how most renewal movements come from the bottom up, not from the top down. We will ground our thoughts in biblical background and explore our Wesleyan roots. We will try to rouse the church to follow the command of Jesus: "Go ... and make disciples."

The church may be sick, but the soul is sick too. Religion may be irrelevant to many, but Jesus Christ and the ways of Christ are not. Certain traditions and cultural forms may be laid aside, but spiritual hunger is deep.

The issue is how to connect. In a spiritually confused and hungry world, how to connect with the Lord, how to connect with a revitalized church. In a mobile, fragmented, isolated population, how to connect with a community of faithful friends. In a cynical, suspicious society, how to find a spot to stand, a place to trust. In a horde of denominations populated by increasingly isolated congregations, how to connect in communication. In a world of deadly disease, famine, and indescribable poverty, how to link arms as Christians to work together in caring ministries.

The issue is deeper, much deeper, than trying to help a denomination grow again. The issue is not merely "religion"; it is "salvation." The ultimate task is drawing people of all ages, all nationalities, all races and ethnic backgrounds, all philosophical persuasions, to the One who said, "I came that [you] may have life, and have it abundantly" (John 10:10).

Our task is to connect—connect with other churches, connect with one another in the church, connect with children and youth, connect with the unchurched, connect with the Savior. We want to sing joyously:

Blest be the tie that binds
Our hearts in Christian love.

Chapter 1 / BACK TO SQUARE ONE

If any want to become my followers,

let them deny themselves

and take up their cross and follow me. (Matt. 16:24)

These may not be the worst of times, but they certainly aren't the best of times—not for our world, not for our country, not for the church of Jesus Christ. Our world festers with disease, famine, and poverty. Our country is engaged in a tragic death scene in Iraq. Many of our churches wander about in decline. I'm tempted to say with G. K. Chesterton, "I've never seen the world so festering with damnation." Many of our churches are disconnected and out of touch—out of touch with the twenty-first century and out of touch with the average man or woman, boy or girl in our towns and cities. What can we do?

My roommate in college was studying to be an engineer. When things went sour or some plan fell all apart, he would say quietly, "Well, I guess it's back to square one." Maybe he had the old game of Monopoly in mind: when you land on a bad square and have to go back to "start." Or maybe his engineer's mind forced him to wad up a set of faulty, messy blueprints, toss them in the wastebasket, and start over. Anyway, he drilled deep in my mind, "Back to square one."

From a more scholarly source, when I studied under H. Richard Niebuhr at Yale, he said something like this: "The great Christian revolutions come not by the discovery of something that was not known before. They happen when somebody takes radically something that was always there."

In the church, it is imperative that we get back to our beginnings. We must remember where we came from, how we got started. We have to reclaim our spiritual roots. The issue is not romance or nostalgia. It is rediscovering who we are. Recovering our vibrant beginnings will energize our return to vitality and growth. But it won't be easy.

Recently I sat down with a group of preachers. They were discouraged. Depressed. "What's wrong?" I asked. They rolled their eyes at me like I was a relic of the Stone Age.

Finally, one preacher spoke up. "The bishop wants me to go to a high steeple church. Big salary. Prestige. Powerful pipe organ playing Bach. Old folks in neckties and dresses sitting in the same pews for the past forty years.

"The children and youth are mostly grown and gone, yet the church building is surrounded by an influx of new families. It is near a university campus, not far from a new residential development. The congregation has been in decline for forty years. The bishop wants me to go in there and turn that church around.

"I told the bishop that the church wants a chaplain to hold their hands while they grow old and die. The bishop said, 'Go in there, wake them up, and make disciples.' Can you imagine me putting up a screen in that neo-Gothic sanctuary? If I brought in a few guitars and a trap drum, the fat would be in the fire for sure. Even if I started a contemporary service in the fellowship hall, I'd have World War III on my hands. What if I told them I wanted every member to be in ministry, facilitating DISCIPLE Bible study and small groups, calling on the sick as Stephen ministers, helping reorganize the children's ministries, leading small clusters of youth, visiting face-to-face with people in the neighborhood?

"If I tried to bring them into the Lord Jesus' ministry in the twenty-first century, I'd either last a year or two and be thrown out, or I'd survive and suffer constant criticism as we tried to make new disciples and if we began to grow."

The pastor leaned back and muttered, "Do I want to pay that price?"

Twenty years ago, I wrote *And Are We Yet Alive* and complained about the 1964–1984 decline in United Methodism: membership, down; worship, down; Sunday school attendance, down. I said then that "we are tired, listless, fueled only by the nostalgia of former days, walking with a droop, eyes on the ground, discouraged, putting one foot ahead of the other, like a tired old man who remembers, but can no longer perform" ([Nashville: Abingdon, 1986], p. 9).

But today, instead of complaining about the denominational decline, the disconnect from people in the twenty-first century, the distance our 1950s church culture has from the young, I want to claim ways our churches can explode once again in spiritual, Christ-centered fervor.

Jesus, Savior and Lord

I was thrilled to attend worship recently when the pastor received twenty-nine middle schoolers into full membership. What pleased me was that the youth each gave a personal testimony of accepting Jesus as their Savior. Some had said "yes" to him at church camp, others on a work team, some in Sunday school or youth fellowship. For them, *confirmation* confirmed their *conversion*!

Revivals aren't what they used to be. I'm preaching a two-day revival this fall—mostly very active church members will attend. Evangelism is even a bad word in some circles. Most of the recent forms of evangelism are passé—camp meetings, Billy Graham crusades, revivals, two-by-two calling. Most pastors preach to the faithful, seldom giving an "invitation" to become a disciple. But Jesus made it clear that a person is not saved by osmosis. "If any of you wants to be my follower, you must put aside your selfish ambition, shoulder your cross daily, and follow me" (Luke 9:23 NLT). Salvation still requires a Savior and a decision to trust and follow him.

But it's now hard to win converts at a soccer game, in a Wal-Mart store, or even in a typical Sunday morning worship service. We have forgotten how to help people get started in the faith, and we often lack a venue in which to do it.

Seminaries aren't very helpful here. At Yale and at Dubuque's Lutheran, Presbyterian, and Catholic seminaries, I studied pastoral care and counseling, sermon formation, church history, and biblical exegesis, but I learned very little about how to help a bystander begin the discipleship journey.

Can you imagine swimming coaches spending all their time teaching strokes and never mentioning how to prepare to spring from the diving board? Or baseball coaches never discussing a proper stance in the batter's box? Nothing significant ever happens unless we begin. We must learn—in our church life today—how to help folks get started.

I was raised in the church. Each Sunday morning I sat with my mom, who taught Sunday school, and my dad, who served on the finance committee. I had been confirmed and was an active member of the youth fellowship.

But one Sunday evening, a student from a nearby college—a young man hoping someday to be a preacher—came to talk to our youth group. I was fourteen. A handful of us sat in the huge sanctuary. The student preacher said, "Jesus is like the North Star. Sailors see many stars, many planets roaming around the sky—but those celestial bodies will lead you astray. Only the North Star is faithful, constant."

Then he said, "If you want to follow Jesus, if you want to sail the ship of your life, guided by the true North Star, then come to the prayer rail. Kneel and give your heart to him and promise to follow him. He will never betray you."

OK, so there's more to Christian theology than that. But as long as I live, I will never forget kneeling at that Methodist prayer rail, in a nearly deserted sanctuary, saying to the Lord Jesus, "I want you to be the North Star of my life." It took a college kid to do it for me.

Some people don't like phrases or words like *born again* or *converted* or *saved*. But life-changing faith commitment has to begin somewhere, at some time. Just because some emotional evangelist jumps up and down on a particular expression doesn't justify our failure to lead people to Christ, to pray for them to know and love him.

After all, Jesus said to Nicodemus, "You must be born again [or born from above]" (John 3:7), and our Lord said, "Unless you are converted . . . you shall not enter the kingdom" (Matt. 18:3 NASB).

John Wesley fathomed God's grace in three forms. *Prevenient grace* means God's love is seeking, searching for lost souls (and so ought we to be). *Justifying grace* is that amazing salvation experience when we are "washed in the blood," forgiven of our sins—when he says yes to us and we say yes to him. *Sanctifying grace* is the work of the Holy Spirit in our hearts for the rest of our lives, "perfecting" us and bringing us into the eternal kingdom.

Too many of our sermons today are aimed at the faithful; too few are aimed at the seeker. Too few opportunities are available for people to kneel down and give their hearts to our Lord. Revivals are gone, Ashrams are diminished, Emmaus retreats are waning. I hear testimonies from DISCIPLE Bible study groups, but they are more often decisions for ministry or Holy Spirit experiences by already believers.

If we are to reclaim our roots, we need to relearn the early church, "Day by day the Lord added to their number those who were being saved" (Acts 2:47). And we must recapture Reformation methods of experiencing "justifying" grace by new converts.

The Bible

Take the Bible. Right now, we're warding off two extremes. I feel like the sheriff at the O.K. Corral. People are shooting at me from both sides. The ultraconservatives on the right fire salvos of "inerrancy" (not a biblical word) and "Every word in the Bible is absolutely true. God wrote it; I believe it; and that's all there is to it." The entire universe, with stars reaching beyond the most powerful telescope, was created in six twenty-four-hour days. These literalists often proof text from favorite passages to support their political biases: women, abortion, evolution, homosexuality.

Sometimes I think the inerrancy fundamentalists don't read the whole Bible. Most of them eat shrimp and pork, and work on the Sabbath, and many divorce their spouses. They certainly don't go to Jerusalem three times a year as commanded by the Torah.

But I'm bombarded from the left as well. Many have reacted to the literalists by ridiculing the Scriptures. Some are professors on college campuses, studying the limestone on the Kansas prairies to see how many millions of years the pastures lay under a vast inland ocean. No six-day creation for them; sometimes not even a Creator. Some are philosophers immersed in relativities. No such thing as absolutes. Some are Bible scholars: if Moses didn't write the entire Torah, if Paul didn't pen Ephesians, then those books can't be authoritative. Some are preachers who were raised by Bible thumpers and have spent a lifetime reacting to those fundamentalist absolutes. John Killinger builds his book *Ten Things I Learned Wrong from a Conservative Church* on this theme: how I studied my way out of a Jerry

Falwell–style of biblical interpretation. Trouble is, Killinger, brilliant preacher and professor, throws the baby out with the bath water. Other writings, novels and poems, and classical literature inspire him as much as does the Bible. He groans under the notion that Jesus died for our sins, and he rejects the hymns of his childhood, such as "The Old Rugged Cross" and "When I Survey the Wondrous Cross." Most uncomfortable with John's Gospel, which emphasizes the Word become flesh, Killinger describes "the fourth Gospel, the most fictional and contrived of all the Gospels" ([New York: Crossroad Publishing, 2002], p. 39).

What a pity those who reject the Bible-thumping demand to "raise your hand if you love Jesus" often turn to an agnostic, even atheist rejection of Jesus the Savior. Some accept Jesus as teacher but not as Lord; many no longer find meaning in the Scriptures at all.

Scholars sometimes confuse our seminarians. We are grateful for higher criticism, lower criticism, and historical analysis, thankful for those who study in Hebrew and Greek. But some scholarly classes argue over which was written first, Mark or Matthew, and never prayerfully study the Sermon on the Mount. Some seminary graduates can say why they think Paul didn't really write Ephesians, but they do not "put on the whole armor of God" (Eph. 6:11). A young seminary graduate who joined my ministry had never even studied the Hebrew Scriptures.

When I was an active bishop, I sent a brilliant young seminarian to his first church—out in the boondocks. After a year, I received a phone call from a deep-faithed farmer, chair of the pastoral relations committee. "We need a new preacher," he said. I was stunned. "But the preacher I sent you is a man of sterling character and was tops in his seminary class," I responded.

There was a long pause and then thoughtful words I'll remember forever, "Could you send us some feller who don't know quite so much about this here syn-op-tic problem?" The young pastor was caught up in scholarship when his congregation wanted the good news of the gospel.

I'm glad my doctor has been to medical school. I'm happy that he can name in Latin the bones, the muscles, the nerve endings. But if I have a diseased gallbladder or a ruptured appendix, I don't want scientific terms. I want that doctor to care about *me*, tell *me* that she or he is going to cut a hole in my belly and take the appendix out—that the bottle they hook up to my arm is full of water, sugar, and antibiotics, and that I should be fine in a few days.

Jewish rabbis discussed the scriptures, read and argued about the meanings. Someone asked a rabbi, "Why do you always answer a question with a question?" The rabbi's answer: "Why not?" As Christians, why don't we abstain from shrimp and pork, as clearly banned in Leviticus (11:4-9)? Because Jesus said, "It is not what goes into the mouth that defiles a person, but it is what comes out of the mouth that defiles" (Matt. 15:11). Why don't we stone to death a man or woman caught committing adultery? Because Jesus knelt down in the dust by the woman caught in the act and said, "Let anyone among you who is without sin be the first to throw a stone at her" (John 8:7).

Those of us in the Protestant tradition remember that Martin Luther—monk, priest, and church reformer—rediscovered the Scriptures, translated them into colloquial German, and, aided by the printing press, made the Bible accessible to the people.

The Wesleyan Way

Those of us in the Wesleyan tradition remember that John Wesley said he "was a man of one book." But he also was an Oxford graduate who studied church history, theology, and languages. He commanded his preachers to "read, read, read." Circuit riders on the prairies often gave out books as well as tracts and Bibles—and semiliterate homesteaders eagerly awaited their coming. Today's Christians can accommodate scientific knowledge with the profound meanings of Holy Scripture. We need not be afraid of Truth.

Bishop Scott Jones, when he was a professor at Perkins School of Theology, wrote *John Wesley's Conception and Use of Scripture* (Nashville: Kingswood Books, 1995). Scripture was authoritative insofar as it reflected the saving grace of Jesus Christ. Scott Jones gently reevaluates Albert Outler's oft-quoted authority as "quadrilateral." First, quadrilateral implies four sides, four sources of authority: scripture, tradition, experience, and reason. But Wesley (and Outler) meant scripture as authoritative, interpreted by reason; scripture as authoritative, interpreted by experience; scripture as authoritative, interpreted by tradition. Not four equal sides.

But Scott Jones goes further than the quadrilateral. Scripture, according to Wesley, must be interpreted by scripture. Here is the place literalists foul up. For example, no man who has been castrated or whose penis has been cut off can enter the temple (Deut. 23:1). Yet Philip the evangelist opens the prophet Isaiah (chapter 56) to the Ethiopian eunuch, baptizes him into Christ Jesus, and sends him back to Ethiopia to begin the Coptic church—the oldest fellowship in Christendom. Philip allows Isaiah and the spirit of Jesus to supersede Torah.

Wesley became adamant in his opposition to eighteenth-century slavery. He knew well Paul's admonition to slaves to "obey your earthly masters" (Eph. 6:5). But he also knew Paul's doxology in Christ, there is neither "slave" nor "free" (Gal. 3:28). One passage of scripture interprets another passage of scripture.

Some churches ban women from the pulpit or the priesthood, quoting Paul shushing the talkative, illiterate women in their newfound freedom in the Corinthian church. They take literally "women should be silent in the churches" (1 Cor. 14:34). But the Corinthian church was in turmoil—free and slaves, kosher and gentile, women letting their hair down, men babbling in tongues. The women were illiterate, had never been to school or synagogue. They were chattering, asking foolish questions. But before we ban women from the pulpit, we must read more scripture. Philip the evangelist had four unmarried daughters who prophesied (Acts 21:10). Mary Magdalene was first to shout "I have seen the Lord" (John 20:18). Paul sent his message to the Romans to be proclaimed in every house church in Rome by his powerful woman deacon, Phoebe (Rom. 16:1). Paul's close friend Priscilla instructed Apollos on how to more accurately reveal Jesus as the Christ (Acts 18:26). When Paul, filled with the Holy Spirit, wrote, "In Christ . . . there is no longer male and female" (Gal. 3:26-28), he clarified his Corinthian comment.

Have you ever wondered why the holiness movement had women evangelists, women preachers, women bishops? I credit it partly to Susanna Wesley, John Wesley's mother. When her husband, an Anglican priest, was away, she filled the Epworth parsonage with her preaching and teaching. We believe that the Holy Spirit falls on both women and men.

"Women should be silent in the churches" (1 Cor. 14:34) is used by those who would keep women out of the pulpit (and away from the altar). (Of course, their Sunday schools would close up shop without women teachers.) President Jimmy Carter, in *Our Endangered Values* (New York: Simon and Schuster, 2006), discusses this issue in his chapter "Must Women Be Subservient?" Over this biblical issue, President Carter led his congregation out of the Southern Baptist Church.

I once met the international president of the Salvation Army, General Eva Burrows, the leader from 1986 to 1993. Imagine a woman heading an entire denomination. In the Salvation Army, normally both husbands and wives are ordained. A deeper truth lies at the heart of biblical interpretation. It refutes both the biblical literalist and the cynical agnostic. It is this: "No one can say 'Jesus is Lord' except by the Holy Spirit" (1 Cor. 12:3). The Bible is authoritative, but our ultimate authority, our final word, is Jesus, the Christ, the word made flesh, our Lord and our Savior.

The Holy Spirit

Our square one, our biblical rootage, is grounded in the Holy Spirit. Pentecost is often called the birthday of the church. Followers of Jesus were just a motley group in prayer in Jerusalem until the Holy Spirit fell upon them—just as Jesus promised (Acts 2).

When Peter preached, he was no longer a sniveling coward lying to a waitress, saying that he was no Galilean: "I do not know the man" (Matt. 26:72). Now, filled with the Holy Spirit, Peter proclaimed the gospel in broad daylight in the crowded streets of Jerusalem (Acts 1:15; 2:14).

We Wesleyans, often called the "holiness people," love to quote John Wesley referring to his Holy Spirit experience at Aldersgate, "I felt my heart strangely warmed." How did so many contemporary churches get disconnected from our deep faith in, our joy in, our dependence on the Holy Spirit? When was the last time you heard a sermon on *how* to receive the Holy Spirit? In many churches, the trinitarian benediction including "Father, Son, and Holy Spirit" is the only mention. Some pastors receive profession of faith from persons without laying on hands and praying for the Holy Spirit. If Pentecost was the birth day of the chuch, getting back to "square one" means re-experiencing the Holy Spirit.

When I was a boy, I was taught that God is a gracious Father. I learned to sing "This Is My Father's World." When I was a teenager, trying to figure out how to steer my life, I gave my heart to Jesus. I learned to sing, "Jesus, Savior, Pilot Me." But I attended college, went to church every Sunday, studied hard in seminary, received ordination, and finally served a church; but nobody told me how to receive the Holy Spirit. So as a young preacher, idealistic, hard-working, frustrated, tired, half sick, I went to an Ashram led by world evangelist, Brother E. Stanley Jones.

He told this story of a preacher coming to him and saying: "I'm afraid of the Holy Spirit. I hear about emotional excesses, pentecostal ravings, holy-roller churches.... I'm afraid."

"Are you afraid of Jesus?" Brother Stanley asked.

"No, no, I'm not afraid of Jesus."

"That's what the Holy Spirit is, the Spirit of Jesus," said Stanley.

Oh, thought the preacher. *Then I don't need to be afraid. I don't need to be afraid of the Spirit of Jesus.*

Then Brother Stanley told us *how.* How do you receive the Holy Spirit? He put it in biblical perspective: Jesus said *"wait"* and you will *receive*—passive language (Acts 1:4). I thought being a disciple meant active verbs—try hard, feed the hungry, preach the gospel, comfort the bereaved, study the Bible. Brother Stanley used passive expressions, "letting go," "relaxing in trust," "letting God be God," "surrendering."

"Surrender" got through to me. When I knelt at that Methodist prayer rail, and people laid hands on my head, I said, "Well, Jesus, I'm turning it all over to you." And the Lord said to me, "Well, it's about time!" I felt the world roll off my shoulders. And I heard the Lord say, "I will be responsible for the welfare of humankind, the fate of the world, the well-being of the universe. All you have to is do is be faithful—and that, Dick, is a man-sized job." My soul was flooded with the peace that passeth all understanding. I received the Holy Spirit as Jesus promised. When and where are people receiving the Holy Spirit today?

Oh, we must reconnect with that power! I saw the Holy Spirit at work in the Lay Witness Movement. I, along with many, received a fresh inner experience of the Spirit in a Walk to Emmaus. Letter after letter comes to me from someone in DISCIPLE Bible study who has finally let go, finally said yes to Jesus, finally surrendered.

Fellowship

Paul was dead serious when he said, "Welcome one another" (Rom. 15:7). We'll discuss loneliness later, but we all know that half the folks on church membership rolls are disconnected from the fellowship. Unchurched people receive invitations to "come to church" the way you and I receive unsolicited appeals in the mail. How do we recapture the culture of caring, the intimacy of fellowship?

Robert Schnase, now bishop of the United Methodist Church in Missouri, has written an exciting book, *Five Practices of Fruitful Congregations* (Nashville: Abingdon, 2007). He recalls his pastorate at First United Methodist Church, McAllen, Texas, how he opened up the congregation to be a hospitable, transforming fellowship.

Schnase wasn't crucified for changing things. He was wise. He tells his experience in his chapter, "The Practice of Radical Christianity." Here's his description of the changes that created an open, disciple-making congregation:

> I served one congregation that wanted to deepen its understanding of hospitality, growing beyond the practical steps recommended by books on evangelism, assimilation, and visitor follow-up. We had the techniques right—helpful signage, accessible parking, trained greeters, and a system of visitor follow-up. But we sought a culture of hospitality that extended into our Sunday school classes, mission teams, choirs, and youth ministry. *I invited ten church leaders to commit with me to a series of lunches for in-depth study and reflection on welcoming people into the Body of Christ.*
>
> In our first session, we shared how each of us had come to be a part of the Body of Christ. We discussed questions such as, who had invited us or brought us to church? Where did we become involved, and what type of service or activity did we first attend? What made us feel welcome?
>
> During another session, we discussed the theological meaning of the church as the Body of Christ and delved into the "why" of invitation, welcome, and hospitality. Why do we invite and welcome people into our midst? . . . We discussed the fundamental purpose for which the church exists—to draw people into relationship with God through Jesus Christ—and how this changes lives.
>
> In one session, we talked honestly about the greatest gifts we had received through the church from our relationship with Christ. People

described how First Church had helped them rear their children, and they recounted tender moments of grace that had sustained them through seasons of grief. They gave God thanks for close friendships formed in the church that had shaped their lives and given them insight for dealing with life's challenges.

Schnase continues his careful analysis:

> In most communities, 40 to 60 percent of people have no church relationship. A majority of our neighbors on the streets where we live do not know the name of a pastor to call when they face an unexpected grief.
> Practicing hospitality is not launching a membership drive for a civic organization or inviting people to join a club in order to enhance revenue through dues.... Hospitality means we pray, plan, prepare, and work toward the purpose of helping others receive what we have received in Christ. Hospitality is more than common politeness to newcomers, name tags for greeters, or a few visitor parking spaces, although these are important.... When the spirit of Christ's hospitality pervades a congregation, then every choir, youth ministry, adult Sunday school class, mission team, Bible study, and outreach ministry regularly asks itself, "How are we doing at inviting others and supporting newcomers into our part of the church family? And how can we improve?" (pp. 15-20)

I wish I had known Schnase's strategy. But I did learn fellowship growth from a key layman when I pastored a declining downtown church. Ben Fletcher, retired from the Federal Bureau of Investigation (FBI), walked into my office. "Do you need any help with evangelism?" he said softly. (Secretly I wondered if he planned to arrest a fellow and bring him in as a new convert.) Wisely, I said, "What do you have in mind?"

"My job with the FBI was mostly on the telephone—calling people, checking records, keeping data. I could do that with visitors and prospective members."

Innocent enough, I thought. Little did I know how sophisticated, how comprehensive he would be. Here was his strategy:

1. Telephone every visitor, every newcomer, every name he could get hold of from Sunday school classes, visitor lists, even the newspapers.

2. Visit with them, warm and personal-like, and get information

about their family, their jobs, their neighborhood (keeping useful records).

3. Then call every relevant church member. "Mrs. Smith, you are teaching the four-year-olds. I've just talked to Mrs. Jones. They're new in town and they have a four-year-old son named Joseph. They seem like a nice family—live at 230 South Oak. I thought you might like to give Joseph a ring and invite him to your class; the number is 872-4568." A little pleasantry. Hang up. Next call. President of men's fellowship is given husband's name, job, family information. Member of adult Sunday school class. President of women's society. Member of adult class (note duplication). Three other children: calls from teachers with information on times and places, data on vacation Bible school or youth fellowship from age-group youth plus teachers.

"I can't believe your hospitality," a mother told me. "We've received seven phone calls—three to the kids. We really feel welcome."

Ben Fletcher was amazing. Not everyone is trained by the FBI. But a similar aggressive plan would enlarge most fellowships.

Personal Morality

The New Testament church, churches of the Reformation, and beginning Wesleyan groups emphasized personal accountability and personal morality.

Which is easier: for an emerging sect to be distinctively moral or for a large denomination to be ethically reborn? Easy answer: a small sect. The young, newly formed has distinctive qualities, built-in accountability, clear and strong emphases. On the frontier, the Baptists didn't dance and the Methodists didn't drink. Both fought the saloons. The Mennonites avoided cosmetics and fancy jewelry and prided themselves on telling the truth. The Quakers, in a world of barter, established the one-price system where your best friend paid the same amount as a stranger. Integrity.

The early Methodist class meetings stressed sobriety. Many in England in the eighteenth century drank too much and fought too much—in the bars and in their homes. So the Methodists asked one another each week how they were doing. They stressed concern for the poor, turning greed into compassion. Class leaders called on each member each week to give money for the destitute. Classes stressed sexual and financial integrity. Early Methodists were told to work hard, be frugal with expenditures, and tithe their earnings. Be honest in your dealings, for "a man's word is as good as his bond." The Methodists also stressed education: Wesley, an Oxford scholar, read the classics and studied the Scriptures in Hebrew and Greek. Circuit riders, pounding the prairies, carried in their saddlebags Bibles, tracts, even books to be given out to Methodist farmers. Colleges were established.

Often these small, intensely Christian faith communities stood toe to toe with the culture. When Abilene and Dodge City in Kansas were famous for the Texas cattle drives, the Methodists preached against the saloons. Preacher evangelists stormed against prostitution, drunkenness, dancing, fighting, and killing. Face-to-face opposition was so intense the First Methodist Church of Wichita was burned to the ground by the saloon patrons. A bullet hole in the pulpit of the Evangelical United Brethren church in Winfield, Kansas, testifies to a drunk cowboy objecting to a fiery anti-liquor evangelist. Unfortunately, this intense personal morality often became legalistic. My grandmother walked out of our church on New Year's Eve because we kids were doing folk dances "in the church."

How can we Christians learn again the clear teachings of Jesus? How, in a sin-sick society, can we be a sober, truth-telling, compassionate people again? How can we regain Christ-centered morality without being judgmental or legalistic?

Sure, some of the intense religious practices drift into moralisms and superficial behavior. Sometimes hypocrisy and self-righteous smugness creep in. Our town has voted out liquor stores, but people drive eight miles away to buy their alcohol. My friend, a Free Methodist, says they are not so strict about women wearing cosmetics as they used to be. A few Amish farmers still plow with horses.

But can Christians today claim essential Christian lifestyles? In giving our hearts to our Savior, in pondering the scriptures, in surrendering to the Holy Spirit, surely we must be different from our secular, sin-saturated culture. What are some bedrock ethical issues?

Consider the body. Methodists have never separated "soul" from "body" as if you could be "spiritual" and let the body do as it wills. (St. Paul harpooned that notion.) Health experts say that sedentary, high-calorie Americans are overweight—60 percent obese. Some say United Methodist preachers are higher—up to 68 percent.

What about sex? The latest studies reported by the Associated Press claim that "nine out of ten Americans, men and women, have pre-marital sex."

We face an onslaught of temptation from alcohol and drugs. My Kansas county is the No. 1 methamphetamine lab area of the state. Buy a few over-the-counter medications and you can make "meth" in a vacant barn.

Alcohol on most college campuses pours like water over Niagara Falls. Social life and beer busts go hand in hand. Yes, I know that St. Paul told Timothy (in an environment where drinking water was impure) to "take a little wine for the sake of your stomach" (1 Tim. 5:23). But young Christians today are clearly choosing between a Christ commitment and an alcohol/drug social scene. The issue is so severe that churches serious about this matter are revving up their social programs to give alcohol- and drug-free parties, festivals, and celebrations.

In a self-serving, secular, have-it-your-way society, Christians, sustained by prayer, scripture, and fellowship, are walking a different path. In small groups, in church school classes, in men's and women's fellowship, from the pulpits, we must again emphasize the moral teachings of Jesus. In use of money and speech, let us be known for our integrity. In care of the body, let us observe that the "body is the temple of the Holy Spirit." In dealing with other people, let us exercise compassion. It's back to square one for churches that want to make a difference.

Social Concern

Those of us in the John Wesley tradition—Wesleyans—have Matthew 25 burned into our souls: "I was hungry and you gave me food, I was thirsty and you gave me something to drink, I was a stranger and you welcomed me, I was naked and you gave me clothing, I was sick and you took care of me, I was in prison and you visited me" (Matt. 25:35-36).

That passionate compassion doesn't make us "liberal" or "conservative." It makes us caring. Unfortunately, some folks think they must choose between prayer, Bible study, and small-group ministry on one hand or helping in the food kitchen or building a Habitat house on the other. We must claim the whole gospel—and reach out aggressively, inviting others to join in.

Sure, Emmaus, DISCIPLE, new classes, and new groups can be evangelistic, but so can Volunteers in Mission (VIM). More and more people, young and old, are finding faith, experiencing joy, even finding the Savior as they join in VIM and other mission projects.

But woe to the church that hammers nails and forgets to pray, that paints houses but neglects the Scriptures. Woe to the church that gives bread to the hungry but never gets intimately acquainted with the poor, never offers them the bread of life. Just as the body needs the soul, so good works need spiritual sustenance. Evangelism and caring for the troubled, the sick, and the needy go hand in hand. We need times and places where a person can be converted; we need times and places where a convert can serve.

Sojourners editor Jim Wallis pleads with the more liberal churches to link arms with the more conservative churches on issues and programs where the Scriptures are clear and where we can agree. Particularly, Wallis lifts up the tragic disparity between rich and poor in the U.S. Can we Christians—Catholics, Protestants, Holy Ghost Christians—look through the same lens at issues that affect the sick and the poor around the world? (See *God's Politics* by Jim Wallis [San Francisco: Harper Collins, 2005].)

What a time for Christian groups to join forces and tackle the malaria and AIDS epidemics! Great foundations like the Clinton and Gates groups are willing to help. I recently assisted others to initiate a conversation between the Clinton Foundation and African United Methodist bishops. The foundation has vast resources; the bishops have an infrastructure that contains little churches, tiny clinics, hospitals, and schools in the villages. What a win-win situation. We may be able to inspire secular and governmental support as we listen to Jesus with one ear and the cries of the world with the other. We have much to offer, plus a Wesleyan willingness to cooperate with all comers when the clear commands of Jesus are guiding us. We must work together and forge ahead in a massive war on disease and famine.

Back to square one means the basics—all of them: intense pondering of scripture, intimate prayer fellowships that cross racial and social lines, and the shaping of personal character (sobriety, sexual discipline, and integrity). As we grab wheelbarrows, paintbrushes, water bottles, and frying pans, we must also look around us for folks we can invite to take the journey of faith with us.

Chapter 2 / A FAMINE
IN THE LAND

For as the rain and the snow come down from heaven,

and do not return there until they have watered the earth,

making it bring forth and sprout, . . .

so shall my word be that goes out from my mouth;

it shall not return to me empty,

but it shall accomplish that which I purpose,

and succeed in the thing for which I sent it.

(Isa. 55:10-11)

They don't know. They don't know anything about the Bible. They know rock stars and sitcom celebrities, but they don't know Matthew from Malachi. For most Americans today, especially those under age fifty, the Bible is an unknown book!

Jay Leno, host of TV's *Tonight Show,* often interviews people standing on a street corner. One night he asked questions about the Bible. "Name one of the Ten Commandments." Silence. Then comes a hesitant answer, "God helps those who help themselves?" Leno then says, "Name the four Gospel writers." Stony silence. Shaking his head in frustration, he asks, "Name the Beatles." As one, the crowd shouts, "Paul, John, George, Ringo!"

George Gallup Jr. and George Barna have conducted studies much more scientific than Leno's. They have discovered that 70 percent of college freshmen cannot name four of the Ten Commandments. Three out of four cannot name the Gospel writers. Their surveys dare not even ask where to find the Lord's Prayer or the Sermon on the Mount. Barna, when he is asked to name the most significant religious changes in our society, claims that fewer and fewer people have any clue what scripture really teaches.

When Dr. Gary M. Burge became professor of New Testament at Wheaton College in Wheaton, Illinois, he was proud to be able to teach in a traditional evangelical, Christian school. He knew the widespread ignorance of scripture in the secular culture, but he would be teaching products of Baptist Sunday schools, Assembly of God youth programs, and Methodist mission teams. "These students are intellectually ambitious and spiritually passionate," he writes.

But for four years he studied the biblical literacy of incoming freshmen. He was appalled. One-third could not put the following in order: Abraham, the Old Testament prophets, the death of Christ, and Pentecost. Half could not sequence: Moses in Egypt, Isaac's birth, King Saul's death, and Judah's exile. One-third could not identify Matthew as an apostle from a list of New Testament names. When asked to locate a biblical book supplying a given story, one-third could not find Paul's travels in Acts; half did not know that the Christmas story was in Matthew or that the Passover account was in Exodus.

Dr. Burge decided to inquire in a different direction. He went directly to high school seniors, kids intensely active in their youth ministries in "strong evangelical churches." His simple twenty-five-question survey revealed: merely 15 percent could place in order the major events of Jesus' and Paul's lives. Only one-third could find the Sermon on the Mount in the New Testament; 80 percent did not know where to find the Lord's Prayer.

DISCIPLE Bible study, like a dentist pulling rotted molars, has drawn out strange stories of biblical ignorance. A young lawyer in Dallas, as he received his first-year DISCIPLE pin, took me aside and told me, "I was baptized as a baby but never went to church until I got married. My wife dragged me to DISCIPLE and put a Bible in my hands. The group leader began by saying, 'Well, let's start easy: Let's open up our Bibles to the book of Genesis.' My mind raced," he said. "I remembered my Latin: 'genari,' means 'to give birth to'! Then I thought, the generator starts my car. I smiled," he said, "and figured that Genesis must be near the front of the Bible!"

A prominent Atlanta businessman sat down in a high-powered men's DISCIPLE group, Bible in hand. The leader, to start on a nonthreatening note, asked each one to tell where he got his Bible. One man said he had his mother's. Another showed his, given to him by his church when he was in the third grade. But one man was noticeably silent. The next morning, he phoned the leader to explain. "You know I didn't say anything last night when you asked where people got their Bibles."

"Yes, I noticed, but that's okay. You don't have to share if you don't want to."

"Well, I was silent because I was embarrassed," the man confessed. "I didn't want to say out loud that I went downtown yesterday morning and bought the first Bible I've ever owned."

The funniest story came out of the heart of the Bible Belt. A woman called her leader the morning of the day DISCIPLE was to begin. She said, "A lady just told me that there are a lot of books in the Bible. Would you please go with me to the bookstore this afternoon and help me, so I get *all* the Bible books?"

Let me ask you a question: Where would they have ever learned the Bible?

I am a fantastic supporter of the public schools in America. I believe every child should have a first-class, top-notch education. All of my family, children and grandchildren, are products of good public schools. My daughter-in-law serves on a local school board.

But for two generations we have not read or taught the scriptures in public schools. Recently I went to my civic club luncheon. I sat beside the superintendent of schools. He stood up and thanked the club for giving a book to every first grader and for donating a dictionary to each third grader in our excellent local school system.

But he didn't thank us for giving Bibles.

But, you say, we have Sunday schools. In my book, *And Are We Yet Alive?,* I described a 20-year decline in the Sunday school. The decline has now continued unabated for over 40 years. In the 1890s we Methodists had more in attendance in Sunday schools than the entire membership of our churches. Our son, Paul, a pastor in suburban Wichita, has to compete with children's soccer leagues that schedule matches on Sunday mornings. Children of broken homes may spend one Sunday with Mom, another Sunday with Dad. In an era of 60- to 70-hour workweeks, Sunday has become the day to play golf, catch a movie, do household chores. Sunday school has dropped far down the list of priorities.

And what about the home? Don't Mom and Dad read the scriptures around the breakfast table? Doesn't Grandpa or Grandma sit by the fireside in the evening reading Bible stories to the grandchildren? Ha! If your family is like ours, it is hard to have a family meal together. The children—with their music, sports, video games, schoolwork, and church activities—are even busier than their parents.

Prophesies Realized

The words of prophetic voices are ringing true. As early as 1934, T. S. Eliot in his Choruses from "The Rock" tells of a wasteland to come:

> Where My Word is unspoken,
> *In the land of lobelias and tennis flannels*
> ·····································
> The wind shall say: "Here were decent godless people:
> Their only monument the asphalt road
> And a thousand lost golf balls."

More profound—and even more frightening—are the eighth-century B.C. words of the prophet Amos:

> The time is surely coming, says the Lord GOD,
>> when I will send a famine on the land;
> not a famine of bread, or a thirst for water,
>> but of hearing the words of the LORD.
> They shall wander from sea to sea,
>> and from north to east;
> they shall run to and fro, seeking the word of the LORD,
>> but they shall not find it.
> In that day the beautiful young women and the young men
>> shall faint for thirst.
> ····························
>> they shall fall, and never rise again.
>> (Amos 8:11-13)

When I first read Amos's words, I thought it strange he would say that without the words of God, people would go "from the north to the east." Usually we say north to south or east to west. Then I looked at the map. You can start in the snows of Mt. Hermon, the beginnings of the River Jordan, the agriculturally rich hills and valleys of Galilee—the north. Then you can turn dramatically and go east—into the desert! The deserts of Jordan, the endless sands of Iraq and Saudi Arabia! A traveler on foot would perish in the wastelands without sustaining, life-giving water—the water of the Word.

The terrible words of Amos should keep us awake at night: "Where my word is unspoken, your beautiful young women and strong young men will fall down. They will fall down and never get up again." You don't have to be a prophet today to see people falling down, never to get up. Consider the following issues.

Integrity

Do you read the morning newspaper or listen to the evening news? List the corporate executives who have lied and cheated. Drive by the Enron building in Houston that stands forlorn and empty. The former CEO of WorldCom is in prison for orchestrating an $11 billion accounting fraud. Do you want to know how many high school and college students cheat on their themes, papers, and tests? Some say 80 percent!

When I was a teenager, I worked summers raising alfalfa hay. We had no cattle, so I would sell the hay to farmers and ranchers. One day a Mennonite farmer bought my hay, shook hands with me, and agreed on a price: $20 a ton in the field. Then he added, "My dog will be in the cab." I was only sixteen, so I told my dad about the transaction. He nodded in agreement with the price, smiled at the handshake, but then grew serious when I mentioned the dog. "What did he mean," I asked, "the dog will be in the cab?" Dad carefully explained that the driver would weigh his truck, empty, and then would weigh it again, loaded with hay. The elevator operator would note on the weight ticket whether the driver was in or out of the truck. But the dog? If the dog were weighed in the empty truck but jumped out of the loaded truck, I would be cheated.

Now, I was only 16, but I started figuring: $20 a ton, a penny a pound. If the dog weighed 27 pounds, I would lose 27 cents. I smiled, but Dad was thoughtful. "He wanted you to know that his handshake meant absolute integrity."

Consider recapturing integrity. Moses told you, "You shall not steal" and "You shall not bear false witness" (Ex. 20:15-16). It's more important for us to plant those commandments in our hearts than to post them at the courthouse. Jesus said, in effect, not to swear on a stack of Bibles, but to "let your 'Yes' be 'Yes,' and your 'No,' 'No' " (Matt. 5:37 NKJV). John's Revelation foresees Jesus the Lord coming with a sword—not a sword in his hand but a sword in his mouth!

Truth—clean, clear, absolute truth (Rev. 19:15). In a church spiritually reborn, the dog ought to be in the cab, both times.

Sex

Or would you rather discuss sex? We don't need Amos to warn us. We live in a society fascinated with sex, fueled by modern sex-image marketing methods and the postmodern worldview that there is no right or wrong.

Half of all marriages in the U.S. end in divorce. We are the divorce capital of the world. Daily we read of distinguished military leaders, high political officials, business executives, and preachers or priests dismissed for fornication, adultery, pedophilia, or sexual abuse. Our sports heroes jump from the sports page to the front page with their sexual escapades.

Sexual experience of youth under seventeen is about 65 percent, and under twenty-one it's about 80 percent, most with more than one partner. The United States has the highest rate of pregnancy among unmarried teenagers in the world. More than one million babies a year are born to unmarried women, more than one-fourth of the total live births in the country. We have twenty-five abortions for every hundred live births, forty per hundred for women under twenty-five. Three times as many adults cohabit before marriage as twenty years ago; some say 80 percent live together prior to a wedding. Yet evidence shows cohabiters have a near 50 percent greater chance of divorce. When these couples do marry, they are "more likely to be victims of domestic violence, depression, dissatisfaction with life, shorter life spans and sexual anxiety" (George Barna, *Singlefocus* [New York: Regan Books, 2003], p. 61).

Barna notes (page 44) that the Centers for Disease Control reports 65 million Americans "carry an incurable sexually transmitted disease (STD). Fifteen million more are infected each year. One of four teens already has an STD." Clearly we have lost our way in building and maintaining healthy relationships.

Drugs and Alcohol

When the Bible teaches that the body is a "temple of the Holy Spirit" (1 Cor. 6:19) the idea is not confinement but freedom, not restriction but health. Saying no to drugs, alcohol, and tobacco is saying yes to vibrancy, zest, and long life.

My grandpa chewed Spark Plug tobacco; he spit in a Folgers coffee can. My dad said it was a filthy habit. I tried it once and quickly gave it up. We now know smoking causes cancer. One reason I don't smoke is that my aunt died of lung cancer; my uncle, of throat cancer.

My college fraternity has, at one time, been on probation for alcohol abuse. Another fraternity was banned from the campus for the same reason. Many people consider partying, drug use, and drunkenness as synonymous. Like Amos the prophet said, some go from the fertile North into the deadly desert. Pondering the scriptures, being immersed in intimate Christian community can help us lead healthy lives.

Death

Do you know the second greatest cause of death among young people aged sixteen to twenty-five? The first cause of death is accidents—often alcohol- and drug-related. But the second major cause is *suicide*—suicide in the freest, most prosperous nation in the world. Lacking spiritual meaning, divine purpose, soul-cleansing forgiveness, "the beautiful young women and the young men ... shall fall, and never rise again."

Prison

Get ready for chapter 11. Over two million Americans are prison inmates—one-fourth of all the prisoners in the world! About six million men and women are under the jurisdiction of the courts—arrested, awaiting trial, in jail, out on bail, on work release, under probation.

Yes, most are from broken homes. Yes, some have reading problems that caused trouble in school. Yes, many are in prison for possession or sale of drugs. Yes, some are mentally ill. But what a tragedy! What a loss of human potential, what a social and financial burden!

Is there no hope? Is there no way the saving grace of God can reach out to those who are falling, never to rise up again? Jesus said

"I am the way, and the truth, and the life" (John 14:6). He said those who hear his words and do them will be like a man who builds his house on a rock (Matt. 7:24). It is up to us to go to the prisoners, teach them, and help them find him who gives life and wholeness. Jesus said, "I was in prison and you visited me" (Matt. 25:36).

Most of all, we'll remember the words of the great German theologian and martyr Dietrich Bonhoeffer, who proclaimed that every great revival in the church has come about through a rediscovering of scripture.

Chapter 3 / LOOK AT ALL THE LONELY PEOPLE

All who believed were together and had all things in common;...

They broke bread at home

and ate their food with glad and generous hearts.

(Acts 2:44-46)

The Beatles saw it coming. Way back in the 1960s, they sang "Eleanor Rigby:"

> Look at all the lonely people
> Where do they all belong?

Today's rap singer ARON beats out the sad and sorrowful song, "I'm So Lonely; I'm So Lonely; I'm So Lonely."

In the 1930s and 1940s, even the 1950s, when I grew up in my little town, Grandma's friends, the merchants, even the policemen, called me by name. My dad, the funeral director, knew everybody. I saw my schoolteachers in the stores. My doctor's wife taught my Sunday school class. Friends of mine who grew up in big cities say they lived in close-knit neighborhoods. People knew each other—bought their meat from the same butcher, played on the streets with kids from families they knew, helped one another when somebody was sick or in trouble, and spoke with the same accent, Italian or Irish or Hispanic.

But times and society have changed. Kids left the farms and small towns to get jobs in the city. Urbanization with its accompanying isolation swept the world. Kansas kids from Dodge City went to Denver, where they didn't know a soul. Young black men left Georgia to get jobs in Detroit.

"Mabel, where's that engineer son of yours?"

"Oh, he got a job with Boeing in Seattle."

"George, where's that beautiful daughter, Sarah, who graduated from high school?"

"Oh, she's married now, has a two-year-old son, and lives in Atlanta."

Mobility—even worldwide mobility—became the order of the day. Now, Christmas letters from old friends tell of faraway grandchildren in places like Brussels or Cairo or Manila. Talk about disconnected family and friends!

When I left my home state of Kansas in 1984, the church sent me as bishop to Arkansas. I went to Little Rock, the capital. Little Rock is located in the center of the state, like the hub of a wheel. Day by day I traveled the state. When I came home at night, I didn't look left or right. I scarcely knew the neighbors next door—even after eight or nine years.

One winter night I awoke from a sound sleep to hear the scream of sirens. I looked across the street, one house over, and saw flames belching from upstairs windows, firemen stretching out hoses. The next morning we learned that our neighbor—an older, single woman, an alcoholic—had accidentally set her house on fire. In a drunken stupor, she dropped a cigarette on the couch. Her house was demolished. She and her dog died of smoke inhalation. I didn't even know her name.

Now, I'm an Anglo-Saxon, white, married, middle-class, educated American citizen. What if I were a single man from Mexico, cutting up chickens in northwest Arkansas, sleeping in a car so I could send two-thirds of my pay back to my family? What if I were a high school dropout from Virginia, working for Wendy's in St. Louis? What if I were a college grad, just married, taking my bride to my first job in Houston, renting our first apartment? Who would I know? Who would be my support group, my friends? I would be desperate to go "where somebody knows my name."

When our daughter, Sarah, took her first job in Dallas, she wrote that she didn't know anybody. How could she make some friends? I suggested she go downtown to First United Methodist Church and look for a Sunday school class of young single adults. Imagine my thrill when she called home excited, saying she found that class and they went out to lunch together after church. "Dad," she exclaimed, "I'm going to make it—I've got some Christian friends!" Unfortunately, not one person in a thousand knows how to take this step.

The scholars and social scientists are nailing down these personal observations with careful data. The Harvard psychiatrist Edward M. Hallowell writes *Connect*. Like an accountant keeping careful books, Dr. Hallowell catalogues friends separated from friends, families disconnected, machinists who don't know the name of the man at the neighboring machine, folks alienated from the church—even from the Lord.

He writes:

> Interpersonal bridges are breaking down.... Just as our highway system needs repair, the interpersonal infrastructure of America is weakening.... For most people, the two most powerful experiences in life are achieving and connecting.... While we are doing well at achieving, we are not doing well at connecting.... We need to connect—or reconnect—to our pasts, our traditions, and our ideals.... Both our health and our happiness depend upon it. (pp. xi-xii)

Do you remember Robert Reich, that small-in-stature, brilliant man who served as Secretary of Labor in the Clinton administration? His statistics in *The Future of Success* come crashing down on us like a snowy mountain avalanche. Many people are working hard, too hard. Women are working outside the home in revolutionary numbers. Connectedness, even in the family, deteriorates ([New York: Alfred A. Knopf, 2001], p. 170).

Dr. Reich puts flesh and blood in his research. He loved his job as Secretary of Labor more than any work he had ever done, but, he declares,

> A few years ago, I had a problem: I couldn't wait to get to the office in the morning and only left at night reluctantly. Being a member of the President's Cabinet was so much better than any job I'd had that I couldn't get enough of it. Not surprisingly, the rest of my life shriveled into a dried raisin. I lost contact with old friends. I saw little of my wife and even less of our two sons, Adam, then 15, and Sam, 12.
>   One evening, for the sixth time in a row, I phoned home to tell the

boys that once again I'd miss their bedtime. That's okay, said Sam. But could I wake him up when I did get home? That would be real late, I said; he would have gone to sleep long before. Sam listened, but insisted. I asked him why. He said he just wanted to know I was there.

At that moment Dr. Reich decided to resign as Secretary of Labor, become a professor again, and rediscover his family and friends. In his research, he insists that he is not an isolated example of frenetic work. Many Americans are so busy that they are disconnected from family, friends, church, even God (pp. 3-4).

In 2000, Harvard sociologist Robert Putnam published his land-mark book *Bowling Alone,* which shows that, for the first two-thirds of the twentieth century, Americans were connecting with one another and with community affairs. He argues that people in the United States used to belong to clubs and such. Ordinary folks joined the PTA, drank a beer at the VFW clubhouse on Friday nights, at-tended the nearby Methodist or Presbyterian church, or belonged to a labor union. They played on a team that bowled in a local league every Thursday night.

But in the 1960s Americans in massive numbers began to join less, trust less, give less, vote less, and schmooze less. Bowling leagues diminished, as did mainline churches, social clubs, and labor unions, by 25 to 50 percent ([New York: Simon and Schuster, 2001], pp. 15-16).

The causes are no mystery. Putnam uses the vocabulary of his pro-fession to describe them. He names "privatization of leisure time that accompanied the explosion of electronic entertainment." (In other words, we stay home to watch TV or play on the computer.) Another reason, he writes, is "labor market changes that drew ever greater numbers of adults out of home-based unpaid work and into long hours of paid employment." (Both Mom and Dad went to work—sometimes at more than one job.) He points to "the suburban sprawl that bifur-cates our communities of residence from our communities of work." (People work in downtown Houston but reside in Sugarland, or they live in Connecticut but ride a commuter train for two hours a day to work in New York City.) No time, no energy is left to volunteer, or to join the Women's Society of Christian Service or the Kiwanis Club. A man or a woman gets off work at 5:00 p.m. Friday, glances at his or her watch and decides there is just enough time to bowl a line or two before dinner—"bowling alone"!

Connecting

What can the church do to connect people once again—connect them with friends, with family, with Jesus, with congregational life? First, let's acknowledge that the soft, gentle methodology of the 1950s is not working. The low expectation "come visit our church sometime" or "if you would like to join the church this morning, come forward as we sing" won't cut it today. And that's if you are white and upper or middle class. Try being a stranger, being new in town, speaking with an accent, working blue-collar jobs, relocating just out of school!

We can learn much from the churches that are succeeding in making disciples, in breaking down disconnectedness, in building community.

First, they acknowledge people's ignorance of scripture. No longer can a preacher stand in front of a congregation, Bible in hand, and say, "I'm reading a familiar passage." Half of the listeners have never read Matthew 5 or 1 Corinthians 13 or Psalm 23. Also, the preacher can no longer preach, as I used to do, making a casual reference to Joseph in jail in Egypt or to the bridesmaids who ran out of oil at the wedding feast. For any reference now—if you are trying to communicate with the unchurched (and with most folks under 50)—you must give the context and tell the full story, or it is meaningless. Disciplemaking churches know how to start easy, then teach and build up knowledge of scripture in a secular world.

Second, aggressive congregations know how to extend warm, personal invitations. In a day of mass advertising by TV and newspapers—even the spam on the Internet—we are bombarded by invites, good news, slogans, and name recognition. Ads in the newspaper, signs on the church, even a regular Sunday worship service broadcast on radio or TV are only a first step. They can establish name recognition. The United Methodist campaign "Open Doors, Open Hearts, Open Minds" causes some to think they might be welcome. It causes others—unchurched—to think, "I guess they want me, like Kroger wants me, to shop there."

Today, about the only thing that works for the inactive, the fallen away, the secular unchurched is the warm, face-to-face personal invitation from a friend—and not "to church" usually, but to some small group meeting, typically in a home. "Church" scares most unchurched people—the building, the robes, the unfamiliar pews, the liturgy (formal or contemporary)—are overwhelming.

A few years back, while visiting London, I turned on the "telly" and watched an hour-long program by the British Broadcasting Company on the Alpha movement. This small group outreach plan of the evangelical wing of the Anglican Church stressed a pub friend inviting another pub friend to his or her home to share ideas and learn about unknown or obscure things like "God" and "Jesus" and "Bible." The sessions are not led by a priest but by a layperson and are carefully designed for the flat-out, don't know a thing, let's talk about ordinary unchurched citizen. Alpha now has swept through aggressive U.S. churches, reaching scores of thousands of people and helping them begin to connect.

Group Life

Robert Putman, of *Bowling Alone,* along with Lewis Feldstein, has written a follow-up book, *Better Together: Restoring the American Community* (New York: Simon and Schuster, 2004). They show ways in which parent groups, civic organizations, businesses, and churches are fighting back. They argue that, against the backdrop of busyness, closed-gate housing, mobility, and isolation, some groups are learning how to connect—how to connect people once again.

Putman and Feldstein know that an individual person cannot achieve much change in society. Most important community tasks require a group effort. They call it "social capital"—people connecting to achieve valuable ends.

If the group is made up of old neighbors and friends, and they decide to do something together, the two writers call it "bonding social capital."

When people have traditional, face-to-face relationships, they are "bonded." *Social capital* means they have money-in-the-bank relationships. Nearby farmers bond together to rebuild a burned-out barn. Friends take turns sitting up with a sick neighbor. The local P.T.A. sponsors a spelling bee or a kindergarteners' trip to the zoo. Community action growing out of established friendships has a warm and fuzzy feeling, a kind of kumbaya cuddliness about it. Tight-knit communities tackle a pollution problem or work together to improve the public schools. Don't knock it. Many of our churches—tens of thousands of them—build mission programs, youth ministries, and help for the homeless on bonded social capital.

But in *Better Together* Putman and Feldstein speak of "bridging social capital." The word *bridge* implies crossing over, reaching the other bank, spanning the divide. So they bridge social differences, span isolation, in order to achieve mutual goals. They bridge to gain power, social capital.

Picture an old, once-strong, white urban church in St. Louis now surrounded by run-down mansions, with black and Hispanic kids playing kickball in the parking lot. Or envision upper-middle-class suburbanites in Plano, Texas, who arrive home in two separate cars from work (with high school kids coming home in their own cars) about 6:30 p.m. ready to plop and watch *Jeopardy* or catch up on their e-mail. How can a creative group be formed in St. Louis or Plano? How can we bridge social capital? How can we lead them from loneliness to fellowship?

Putnam and Feldstein give suggestions. They acknowledge that bonding is easier than bridging, but they show how powerful bridging can be when it works. For example, a compelling community problem like a subpar school can draw together folks of different social classes to work for change. A water-resource crisis can cause rich and poor, black and white to link arms and demand action. If people perceive a common interest, a unifying purpose, a heartfelt need, they can bridge cultural and social gaps and become a unified and forceful community.

The church of Jesus Christ ought to understand bridging. Consider the ancient church in Corinth, Greece, a cosmopolitan, seaport city. Who lived in Corinth? People flooded Corinth from all over the world. There were 800,000 slaves and 400,000 free. Wealthy Greek merchants and Jewish Rabbis. Sophisticated Greek philosophers. Take former kosher Jews, Greek patriarchs, slaves of every nation in the Roman empire, women unused to social forms, put them all in the same room, add a dose of Holy Spirit enthusiasm, even speaking in tongues—and what do you have? Confusion, yes. Disharmony, yes. But also gospel-driven outreach to bring people to the Savior. Inspired by the gospel and by love within the fellowship, they "bridged social capital" in order to evangelize the city and beyond.

The picture could have been depressing. St. Paul must have often wrung his hands. Look at the scene: rich people eating all the food before the slaves got off work, men wearing hats in church, gluttons getting drunk on the Communion wine, unschooled women letting their hair down—all constantly babbling questions to the leaders, arguing over whether Apollos or Paul was the better preacher. No wonder St. Paul wrote 1 Corinthians 12 urging people to use their different gifts, and 1 Corinthians 13 pleading with the people to love one another! And they did. They found unity in Jesus, the gospel, the Holy Spirit—and in the huge task of making new disciples. They bridged social capital to spread the faith all around the Mediterranean.

If the early church could get over kosher food, Sabbath legalism, temple worship, and racial bias, surely we can relearn how to bridge. Remember, Paul shouted out, "He is our peace," he "has broken down the dividing wall, that is, hostility between us.... You are no longer strangers and aliens, but you are citizens with the saints and also members of the household of God" (Eph. 2:14, 19). Paul knew how to bridge social capital. "There is no longer Jew or Greek, there is no longer slave or free, there is no longer male and female; for all of you are one in Christ Jesus" (Gal. 3:28).

Grouping for Intimacy

The word *fellowship* belongs to the church. Early Christians stole that word (*koinonia*) from the secular world. It means "sharedness." Two Greek brothers would inherit land and farm it together—*koinonia*. Two people would jointly own and run a business together—*koinonia*. The Gentile doctor, Luke, in Acts 2:42, says that the early Christians "devoted themselves to the apostles' teaching and fellowship [the 'koinonia'—the sharedness of life together], to the breaking of bread and the prayers." They sang, they prayed, they ate in one another's homes. They made sure each other's needs were met. Imagine the intimacy, the tears, the prayers if a Jewish Christian husband were dragged off to prison. No wonder a crisis erupted when some widows were shortchanged in the food distribution (Acts 6). Christian intimacy is not an end in itself: we are nurtured, held accountable, and inspired in *koinonia* in order for us to serve a needy world and help others find the Lord.

Consider Hispanics. They say that recent years have brought forty-nine or so million people from Latin America into the United States. Northwest Arkansas employs them in the chicken processing plants; western Kansas hires them by the thousands to butcher cattle. The politicians argue over legal and illegal immigration, but the Christian churches see immigrants as children of God.

They are tough to reach. Some sleep four to a room—or in their cars—to save money. I sent a Mexican missionary pastor to northwest Arkansas, and I asked him where he found prospects for his fledgling church. "In two places," he said. "In Wal-Mart buying cheap clothing, and in the Post Office, sending money home to their families."

Language and culture are barriers. Like the Korean immigrants, older folks speak their native language; their children are speaking English. American church culture seems strange to them. Some are baptized; some are not. Most are not involved in any church, Catholic or otherwise.

Lake Highlands UMC in North Dallas decided to recruit Spanish-speaking laypersons to lead small Bible study groups in the strip mall where they worked. They developed half a dozen regular groups. Then one of their Spanish-speaking staff supervised them and began to lead a tiny worship service in the chapel on Sunday. They are gradually integrating these new Texans into the life of their congregation.

In Liberal, Kansas, the Reverend Ken Hathaway was approached by a Mexican member wo wanted to rent the chapel for a Spanish-speaking service. "Why, no," he said. "This is your church, let's just do it." Obtaining an associate who spoke Spanish, they began on Sunday afternoon in the chapel. But many had to work on Sunday—the cattle industry never rests—so they began a Thursday night service. On Wednesday night the Hispanic women volunteered to fix dinner for the church before the Disciple studies, youth gatherings, and children's activities got underway, and everyone got acquainted. The money the Hispanic women make they give to support two destitute families. Fellowship can happen, even across cultural and language lines, if the spirit is willing.

In Wesley's England, almost every citizen was a baptized, registered member of a parish. But they were not a part of the body, the fellowship. John Wesley quickly saw that neither he nor his brother, Charles, nor the evangelist George Whitefield could minister adequately to the new converts. So he developed the "Wesley Class Meeting"—a dozen or so folks gathering in somebody's home to pray and to hold each other accountable for being sober, paying their bills, studying the Bible, being in prayer. They shared life together. What made the bridge? The experience of Christ's love; the challenge of growing Christlike; the hope of eternal salvation. They were wildly diverse too: Oxford scholars and illiterate miners, socially prominent citizens and people of the streets, townspeople and farmers. They met to grow in faith and gather strength for their Christian walk.

One day, when DISCIPLE Bible study was being created, I drank a cup of coffee with the noted Wesley scholar, Dr. Albert Outler. I blurted out, "Dr. Outler, we need Spirit-filled, on-fire preachers today—preachers like Wesley and Whitefield." Patiently, Outler put down his cup and said gently, "Dick, that's true, but remember, more conversions took place in the Wesley class meetings than under the preaching of the evangelists." The preacher in me was taken aback, offended a little, so I asked, "What do you mean?"

"Here's what happened," he said. "As Wesley was preaching, the Methodists would work the crowd. They would spot a woman with tears streaming down her cheeks, or a man leaning in, a hand cupped to his ear, and the Methodist would ask, 'Do you understand what you are hearing?'"

"'No, we've never heard anything like this before,' they would respond.

"Then the Methodist would say, 'Come to Joe's house Thursday night and we'll talk about it.'" Then Dr. Outler drove the point home. "At Joe's house, they gave their hearts to Jesus Christ, they surrendered to the gift of the Holy Spirit, they prayed, studied Scripture, held each other accountable for their daily actions, and witnessed to others."

We've discovered in DISCIPLE Bible study groups that great spiritual power is found in diversity. Whereas we often create an adult Sunday school class with people of similar age and interest, DISCIPLE creatively crosses social barriers. Older women in upstate New York told me of the seventeen-year-old boy who joined their group. The women would have one interpretation of a scripture passage—and the boy would say, "Oh, I thought it meant . . ." The women found it a rich experience.

Our son, Paul, led a DISCIPLE group in his Houston home with a diversity of incomes, races, and ages. I wish you could have seen the togetherness, the *koinonia* the night Paul was ordained. After the service, after the reception, they burst into his home near midnight, bringing hugs, ice cream and cake, songs and prayers. Talk about loneliness dispelled; talk about bridging social capital; talk about diversity transformed into love support!

I received a letter from West Virginia, from a woman unknown to me. I read with interest as she said one of the members of her DISCIPLE group wanted to include a young, pregnant, unmarried woman. The nine months of DISCIPLE study and pregnancy passed. The baby was born. I began to weep as I read, "I wish you could have been in church Sunday as our DISCIPLE group stood around the baptismal font. We baptized the baby and then we baptized the mother—with tears of joy running down our faces!"

In a recent prison DISCIPLE group I noticed, as we got started, that the group was diverse: Hispanic, white, black, aged seventeen to fifty-two. One had a master's degree; another could scarcely read. Three of us were "outsiders"; the rest were "insiders." But week by week, categories became people, and people became persons, and persons became souls, and souls became spiritual friends. We prayed for each other daily and called one another by name. The Holy Spirit, the work of Jesus Christ in our midst, broke down the barriers. As we studied and shared each week, we became a close-knit fellowship, a group of Christian friends. We help them find a church home, a job, and a place to live when they are released from prison. We stay in touch.

When we study growing churches we must be careful lest we miss the key point. We can talk about their culturally friendly worship services. We can jump up and down about their trap drums and electric guitars. We can rave about their available parking, their "no offering plate for visitors" policy. We preachers can, and should, study their sermons. But we will never understand their growth, their spiritual staying power, until we comprehend their commitment to developing intimate relationships. They have learned how to bridge, how to build *koinonia* through small group experiences. They invite, personally, newcomers and outsiders to be a part of a small group, and miracles begin to happen. They help lonely people connect.

Robert Putnam, in *Better Together*, devotes an entire chapter to

Saddleback Church in California. The pastor, Rick Warren, is the author of *The Purpose Driven Church* and *The Purpose Driven Life*. OK, so Rick Warren is a bit Calvinistic; yes, his Baptist roots show sometimes; of course, he's Californian with sport shirts and sneakers—but don't get distracted. He teaches, preaches, promotes, and stresses day in and day out, that Christians—beginners, folks who are growing spiritually, serious veterans of the faith—must be in small, face-to-face, *koinonia* groups. He grabs their common interest—to find the purpose for their lives. That purpose cannot be fulfilled in lonely isolation, for as John Wesley said, "There is no such thing as solitary religion." And Jesus said, "Where two or three are gathered in my name, there am I in the midst of them" (Matt. 18:20 RSV).

Chapter 4 / ADULTS

They spent their time in learning from the apostles,

taking part in the fellowship, and

sharing in the fellowship meals and the prayers.

(Acts 2:42 GNT)

Pollsters George Gallup Jr. and D. Michael Lindsay, experienced experts on taking surveys and long-time students of church affairs, argue that churches should take surveys too. Like a veteran shoe salesman showing a young boy how to tie his shoes, Gallup carefully explains how congregations can study the thoughts and feelings of their own members and then explore the attitudes and potential receptivity of their surrounding or constituent communities.

In their book *The Gallup Guide: Reality Check for 21st Century Churches* (Loveland, Colo.: Group Publishing, 2002), Gallup and Lindsay provide face-to-face interview questions, sample telephone interviews, and mail-out questionnaires. They give powerful success stories. Best of all, they explain why to do it: "Churches of America, in these opening years of the twenty-first century, face an historic moment of opportunity. Surveys record an unprecedented desire for religious and spiritual growth among people in all walks of life.... There is an intense searching for spiritual moorings, a hunger for God" (p. 7). "The percentage of Americans wanting spiritual growth has shot up from six in ten, to eight in ten in the last decade" (p. 8).

But local research is needed to help church leaders ascertain where people are in their religious and spiritual growth process. Many people are trying a "do it yourself" and a "whatever works" kind of religion. Religious faith is "broad but not deep" (p. 8).

A survey of church members in many denominations will show a lack of knowledge about their faith traditions. Gallup claims that "only 13 percent of Americans have what might be called a truly transforming faith" (p. 8). They do not know their basic Christian beliefs or the history of their religious traditions.

What a challenge! Finding out what our congregants feel, think, and believe will be a huge, though not impossible, task. Then, discovering the spiritual interests and needs of the unchurched, attacking those needs, and connecting with those guests will require Spirit-filled enthusiasm, planning, and follow-through.

Kenneth Kantzer describes the challenge: "No church can be effective to bring clarity and commitment to a world when it is as ignorant of its own basic principles as is our church today. And unless we engage the church in a mighty program of re-education, it will be unable to transmit a Christian heritage to its own children or the society around it" (Jo H. Lewis and Gordon A. Palmer, foreword by Kenneth S. Kantzer, *What Every Christian Should Know* [Wheaton, Ill.: Victor Books, 1989], foreword).

Christians today must be like a group of King David's soldiers, called the "men of Issachar." They "understood the times and knew what Israel should do" (1 Chron. 12:32 NIV). We too must understand the times, both within the church and outside the church. A congregation not only must find out what its own people know and believe, but also must explore the thoughts of its neighbors. After discovering that, the mighty task of education, evangelism, fellowship, and mission can begin.

Constituency

The question quickly rises: we ask, like a schoolboy on the front row waving his hand: Who and where is our unique constituency—the people God wants us to reach? In the exploding suburbs, the answer is relatively easy. It's everyone in the sprawl of new homes—thousands of them. The strategy often is to start a new congregation, and that requires planning, early on, and lots of it.

Once, in Arkansas, where we were beginning some new congregations, I complained to the Roman Catholic bishop how expensive land was. He responded that Catholics needed quite a bit of land for churches with parochial schools, so they tried to buy land twenty years in advance, before the landowners started selling it by the square foot. Wow! Then I asked a layman friend who bought land for prospective Wal-Mart stores how he knew where to buy. He said that studies by school districts, realtors, and city planners were readily available. Then I noticed a newly built Wal-Mart store they were shutting down and another they were building in a nearby location. "Oh," he said and smiled. "We sometimes make mistakes."

I once pastored a mission church started by an old preacher who just called house to house and started a worship service in a garage. Today, experts suggest a team of a pastor and twenty or thirty laypersons, usually volunteer "missioners" from existing churches, committed folks dedicated to holding small group meetings in their homes. When worship services finally begin, often three to six months later in a school building, the preacher needs a small staff, including some musicians. The idea is to have several hundred people at the first worship service.

Experts say the denomination should buy the land—lots of it—but the congregation should pay for the buildings. The biggest mistake I made was failing to have an available meeting place for the fledgling congregation. Many Arkansas cities passed ordinances refusing worship in school buildings, so some of our groups met in stores or warehouses—then fizzled out for lack of growth space. I tried to get one group to meet in a funeral chapel—like Church of the Resurrection first did in Kansas City—but they refused.

My friend Bishop Robert Fannin wanted to start a new fellowship in an exploding new area near Huntsville, Alabama. He hired a New York consultant who said they should call the worship service "Cappuchino and Christ." The bishop objected, saying that, at least, Christ should come first. But the consultant held firm, arguing that the secular world knows more about cappuccino than it does about Christ. So plans went forward, and the vital new fellowship, "Cappuccino and Christ" at Trinity United Methodist Church now has several thousand in worship.

The Neighborhood

The tragedy of most congregations is that they are spiritually schizophrenic: one mindset on Monday through Friday, another on Sunday.

On Monday noon they eat at a Chinese or Mexican restaurant. On Tuesday they pick up some things at Wal-Mart, paying the black lady at the counter. On Wednesday they take a night class from a professor or teacher who is a lapsed Roman Catholic or burned-out fundamentalist. On Thursday, they have a repairman work on their electrical system. He has a slight accent: a young, second-generation fellow from Honduras. Then on Friday they sit at a football game or soccer match and see persons they've never seen before.

But, on Sunday, they meet their old friends at their dying church, and they wonder why no one new ever comes to worship.

Our daughter, Sarah, a professional church worker, was asked by her bishop in Dallas to help old, dying, inner-city churches come back to life. Once they were several-thousand-member congregations flourishing in prominent, white, upscale neighborhoods; now they were down to fifty or sixty in worship and the neighborhoods had become low-income communities of Hispanics, Asians, and African Americans. Now the beautiful, big, old brick structures are surrounded by kids playing kickball in the parking lots, blue-collar workers, and young immigrants. Like an old bookkeeper moving from an adding machine to a computer, the churches didn't know how to interact with their changed neighborhood, which was basically unchurched.

Sarah decided to reach the adults through the children. So, working with a few old inner-city churches, she helped

- make the church playground officially accessible
- bring in college students to lead after-school and summer children's programs
- rent out a section of the building to social service agencies such as Head Start or charter schools.

Only then did they begin a Spanish-speaking worship service in the chapel. Only then did they call house to house, telling of vacation church school, Sunday school, youth fellowship, and diverse morning worship services.

New Adult Classes

When I went to First United Methodist Church in Wichita, Kansas, I asked myself, "Why would anyone drive past twenty or thirty churches to come all the way downtown?" Answer: "To see their friends!" That meant class groups. They already had a number of large adult Sunday school classes, but they desperately needed to start some new, younger classes. They didn't teach us in seminary how to start new adult Sunday school classes. We had to learn the hard way, but we did, and we developed one of the largest adult Sunday schools in the denomination—all in an historic downtown church.

Our strategy will work for almost any congregation. But as my dad would say, there is a right way and a wrong way. And the air is saturated with false notions. Here are some of them:

Myth: We already have several adult Sunday school classes. Everyone is welcome. We don't need any more classes.

Reality: Adult classes, after a few years, become like family reunions. Strangers might be invited, but they feel like outsiders. A good class has years of shared history together. It's tough to break in.

Myth: There's always room for one more.

Reality: Even adult classes are soon "full." Adults under fifty years of age want discussion, so a class size of fifteen or twenty people is often considered big enough.

Myth: Sunday school is at 9:30 a.m.

Reality: When a congregation begins additional worship services—say a contemporary service at 9:30 a.m.—it must pre-plan for adult classes at 8:30 or 11:00 a.m. or else the schedule will undermine the Sunday school and have some families merely attending worship. People who work on Sunday will even need a group or class that meets at some other time than Sunday morning.

Myth: Announce a class, recruit a teacher, and folks will show up. In other words, "build it and they will come."

Reality: An adult Sunday school class is a small congregation. To launch a class requires planning, recruitment, energy, relationships, structure.

As pastor in Wichita, Kansas, I asked, "How many adult classes do we have?"

Answer: "Thirteen classes for all ages."

"When was the last class formed?" I continued.

They couldn't remember. "We have a young adult class named Hand in Hand that formed about fifteen years ago." Sure enough, those folks were in their midforties and the class had been stable for years.

So we started targeting people over eighteen—singles, students, young adults (married and single), older adults. With new classes we did not use names that implied you had to be married, like 50-50 or Double Ring. We did not want people to feel they were not welcome if they were single.

My wife, Julia, organized a new young adult class. They named it Pneuma—no single or married implications—and Pneuma required a little "spirit" explanation to new members. It is still going strong after over a quarter of a century. Class after class was organized until we had about twenty-five classes of different flavors and different styles—over eight hundred adults in attendance in Sunday school.

In the process, Julia developed guidelines for starting a new class. Here is the strategy:

Bring together a handful of interested persons to pray for the new class. Identify a target area based on age, interest, or need.

Search for names of prospects. Study church and prospective rolls and utilize knowledge of the community. Plan an informal gathering in the pastor's home—a dessert gathering, hamburger fry, or coffee hour.

Have the nucleus telephone or personally invite all prospects to the gathering. Tell people to invite others. Use churchwide—sometimes citywide—publicity: pulpit, newsletter, newspaper, radio, television, and so forth.

Obtain "missionaries"—two or three faithful, caring church people—to help start the class and be a part of it for six months to one year. (They can go to their own class's socials and return to their own class when they finish their mission.) New classes, even though they are made up of adults, don't know how to function. So the missionaries fix the coffee, keep the attendance, take the collection, arrange the socials, telephone absentees, and call on new prospects—all the time guiding other class members. But they don't teach the class. A solid, dedicated teacher (pre-chosen) is a must.

Have the curriculum ready to go. No decisions are made by class members. Later, after some months, they can choose their studies, but not at first. Have a room and a time fixed. Multiple worship services make possible multiple uses for rooms. (Some churches now have great 8:30 and 11:00 a.m. classes.)

At the get-acquainted social, before the first class, meet the pastor, the teacher, and the missionaries. Pass around a paper for their names and the names of other prospects. Ask members to invite others. The missionaries need to call the prospects as well. The first class meeting must be the Sunday immediately following the social.

Follow up with telephone calls by a contact committee and the missionaries. Meet every Sunday without fail, even if only a few are present. Let the class choose a generic name. Avoid age and marital designations. Slowly begin to identify leadership gifts for small responsibilities, modest assignments.

Plan another social within a month. Use missionaries to guide it. Gradually build complexity: prayer concerns, a worship center, devotions, a pianist and a song leader, greeters, a social committee, a class history (scrapbook) person. A job for everyone will build accountability and help bond the group. Take offerings, but keep a class treasury for mission projects.

Plan a service project for the church or community within six months. Have a pastor drop in periodically to say hello. Be alert for those who desire baptism, church membership, or infant baptism, or who have health concerns. Hang steady: you are giving birth to a baby! Plan on two years before the class has the maturity to be self-sufficient.

Continually instill concern for others—people who are hungry for the fellowship they have to offer. Find them. Invite them. Recognize the class in the worship services. Integrate the members into the total fellowship—celebrate and praise the Lord!

Singles

In the "old days" many youth dropped out of church in their late teens, spread their wings for a few years, then by age twenty-two or twenty-five they married, had a baby, and came back to church. Today's world is radically different. Women as well as men go to college, get jobs, join the armed forces, move about, live together for a while, delay marriage until the late twenties or early thirties. They are single for a long time. Add those who are divorced, never married, or widowed, and you have millions of singles in America.

George Barna, *Singlefocus,* in surveying the single scene declares that:

- The U.S.A. holds the highest divorce rate on the planet.
- The number of single parents in the U.S. exceeds the combined populations of Colorado and Tennessee.
- We have more single adults living in the United States than any other nation in the world except China and India. (Our singles exceed the total population of 181 nations.)
- The never-been-marrieds, eighteen years and older, number about 48 million.
- There are more widowed people in the U.S. than the entire population of four dozen other nations (pp. 7-8).

When churches decide to tackle the "single world," they quickly learn singles are not all alike. Some are in college—a different lifestyle than young working adults. Some are not seriously dating, some are living together but postponing marriage (today, about 80 percent live together before marriage). Some are divorced with small children; some are older, divorced after the children are grown. Widows and widowers are all ages, but, with increasing longevity, lots of older folks are single and alone. The experts anticipate a doubling of the over-sixty-five population in the next thirty years.

Now consider the plight of being a single mother. You can imagine how challenging and exhausting it is to be a single mom, one of ten million women who simultaneously serves as sole parent, chief breadwinner, head of the household, and friend to others. As a group they hover near the poverty line with incomes of $25,000 a year, 35 percent below the national household average. For minority singles it is worse, with an average income of less than $20,000 a year.

So when a church envisions ministry with singles it needs to think "variety" like spring flowers in a pasture. Or think of Peter in the resurrection appearance with Jesus. When Peter cast his net on the other side of the boat, he caught 153 fish—of all varieties (John 21:11). We can't lump singles. Not only are they unique individuals of all sizes and shapes, but they come in more varieties of age, experience, interests, and spiritual discernment than we can count. To think that all single adults are alike, and thus to relate to them in an identical manner, is a grievous mistake.

My wake-up call went like this: we asked a dedicated couple to begin a college-age class. Week after week they waited faithfully at 9:30 a.m. Nobody came (in a city with a huge university and several colleges and vocational schools).

One day I asked Steve Wilkins, the young man who directed our youth ministries, if we could have a visit—say Thursday evening. "That's not a good night for me," he said.

"You don't have a junior high or senior high gathering on Thursday, do you?" I replied.

"Oh no, Thursday I have some college kids over to my apartment for Bible study. They would rather stay up late at night than get up on Sunday morning."

"Well, how about meeting before or after that? What time do you meet?"

"Oh, we begin about 8:00 p.m. and I have to kick 'em out about 11 p.m."

"What do you do?" I asked in amazement.

"We sit on the floor, with a Bible in one hand and a soda in the other."

"How many students do you have?" I asked.

"Oh, about twenty," he said—and I fell all apart. Later, some of the students started coming to church; still later, with faith commitments, they struggled out of bed and formed a 9:30 a.m. college class. Several entered the ministry. But it began because Steve knew his clientele, their interests, and their time schedule.

Consider older singles: Sylvia Dewey was a preacher's widow when she came to me saying she was lonely and isolated and didn't feel at home in existing groups. So we formed W.H.O.—Widows (and Widowers) Helping Others. Before long they were eating lunch together after church each Sunday.

When I was a pastor in Wichita, my bishop remembers the morning I called him and asked for an associate. "I only have one request," I said. Silence. "This minister must have been divorced." Dead silence. Then the bishop said, "Dick, I've had a lot of requests, but never one like this." I explained that I wanted to reach singles, especially those who had gone through a divorce. He appointed Doug Morphis, who has now celebrated over a third of a century of ministry to singles with a variety of classes and groups plus Thursday night gatherings called TNT (Thursday Night Together).

Singles in the twenty-first century are a tough bunch to reach. They are busy, immersed in work and play, spiritual but not religious, mobile, often defensive about a divorce or living together or having a partner—not to mention racially, ethnically, and culturally diverse. But they are all children of God. Churches that are good at making new disciples are organizing entrance-level groups that get people started. Alpha and the DISCIPLE eight-week studies are introductory—designed for both singles and marrieds, preparing people for adult Sunday school classes, or for DISCIPLE Bible study, Christian Believer, JESUS AND THE GOSPELS, or other small group life.

Mission

Many singles respond to a task challenge. The experts say many are looking for adventure, for excitement. Mission trips in this country and beyond give meaning to those who are recovering from the death of a loved one or a divorce. Young adults want to participate. Remember Gallup's slogan: *today people must belong before they believe.* Many people are drawn to a task before sitting in a pew. Put hammer and nails in the hands of some single men and women in a Habitat for Humanity project or a trip to New Orleans and you may have a convert.

Don't forget unique needs and problems. Your church may have to put on glasses to see people, single or not, who are alcoholics, drug addicts, or smokers, people who are overweight, physically or mentally handicapped, or on prison work release. Whether it is Alcoholics Anonymous or Weight Watchers, such "comrades in arms" are God's instruments of healing.

Each congregation is unique, every setting different. But churches with a passion to make disciples can ask penetrating questions, targeting age, interests, and spiritual need. Sometimes a mutual interest will aid in breaking a racial or social barrier. In one tiny community, three churches formed a "divorce recovery group" and reached low-income, new-resident Hispanics and upper-income, longtime Anglos in a common search for healing. Churches have started "post-prison" groups that cross racial and social barriers.

I understand that Rick Warren pioneered a powerful therapeutic program called Celebrate Recovery. He involves all sorts of "recovery" people—people struggling with alcohol, drugs, obesity, divorce, death and dying, rejection, and prison experiences, as well as others. Friday night starts at Saddleback Church with supper, followed by a full-blown worship and praise service. Everyone praises God for life, for healing powers, for recovery that is taking place. The twelve-step concept of Alcoholics Anonymous infiltrates the praise service. Then congregants break into small therapy groups, adult groups focused on their individual issues, led by a recovering addict in their area of struggle. The groups are like miniature AA meetings with the gospel added, the testimony, prayer, and "Praise the Lord." What a model of Christian healing!

Recently I went to Long's Chapel United Methodist Church on a Thursday night. They have adopted the "Recovery of Hope." So, I understand, has Cokesbury United Methodist Church in Knoxville, Tennessee. Across the years, I've attended some AA groups, Al Anon groups, Weight Watchers meetings, and marriage therapy sessions—but the mood, the culture here is different.

As they bring in food for the potluck supper, and later as they begin to sing with the small praise band and start to pray, I am impressed with the diversity of social status, ethnic background, and educational diversity—and I am equally impressed with the grace and acceptance they show one another.

As the prayers and testimonies begin, I note the spiritual emphasis, the assurance that Christ Jesus can help them break their addictions. No wonder people from "Recovery of Hope" not only begin to break addictions but also start to join the church.

Another creative ministry for adults called Crossroads Ministry springs out of the rapidly growing Snellville United Methodist Church in the suburbs of Atlanta, Georgia. Guided by Allen and Jewell Merringer, retired businesspeople, Crossroads seeks out-of-work people—people who are often blue, discouraged, even despondent. The Merringers give morale-boosting classes, teach how to write resumes, show the best ways to interview, and hold job fairs. They help connect men and women with training opportunities with both private and public agencies. The Merringers say that the spiritual nurture is the most important part of all!

Some churches target age groups, others explore an interest area. Large churches continually initiate a host of interest groups. If the door is open, you never know who might walk in.

Gifts and Graces

The church reborn will require total participation. Like sailors aboard ship in a crisis, the church cries out "all hands on deck." Help people find a handle for their work and witness. Strip the big committees—it doesn't take sixty people all evening to decide to give the preacher a 3 percent cost-of-living raise. The trustees can hire a plumber to fix the women's toilet or fix it themselves.

Now we need the entire body of Christ to be in ministry. In a disciple-making, Christ-serving congregation, so much ministry is waiting to be done.

St. Paul alluded to the human body to undergird unity, love, and mission. Not everyone is a hand or a foot or a kidney, but all have a part to play (1 Cor. 12). Paul didn't say it, but we know we have to exercise all the parts of the human body regularly. That's why we go to the gym and "work out." "Use it or lose it."

But Paul had more in mind. The body has many functions. All parts are essential and they are quite different. We have our spiritual unity: "No one can say 'Jesus is Lord' except by the Holy Spirit" (1 Cor. 12:3), but we have our multifaceted ministries. Some can teach, some call on the sick, some can visit newcomers. Some churches survey all members each year to discover interests and abilities—spiritual gifts and graces.

I recall visiting Kirbyjon Caldwell's Windsor Village Church in Houston. I wanted to witness his marvelous blend of traditional black gospel participation and emotional expression on one hand and sophisticated analysis, organization, and expression on the other. To my surprise he invited me to join him mid-service as he received new members—folks who had made commitments weeks earlier and had attended membership training. He handed the microphone to each person individually and asked that person to express what his or her ministry was going to be.

An attorney in her thirties said she would remain active in the singles group that had attracted her to the church, but she also wanted to assist with the free legal aid ministry for the poor. A seventh-grade boy said he wanted to sing in the church's teen gospel choir. So it went. Become a Christian. Join the body. Perform your unique ministry.

John Ed Mathison at Frazier Memorial United Methodist Church in Montgomery, Alabama, pioneered the concept of identifying and utilizing gifts and graces. Each January, all the members re-think their spiritual gifts and identify a place where they would like to serve. One Saturday when I was visiting the church I spotted an older man working diligently in the flower beds in front of the sanctuary.

"Who's that?" I asked.

John Ed answered, "You won't believe it. That's the bank president. We were going to ask him to serve on the finance committee, but he said he works with figures all week long and he loves gardening. He asked if he could keep the church's flower beds."

We're in a cultural bind. Folks are busy, yet they want to be connected. They are willing to help if it fits their interests and abilities, but at first they don't want to commit very much time. The days of women giving near full time to church work are over. The times when men would sit for endless hours at a committee or board meeting have ended. Now, the task must be meaningful, relevant, and, usually, short-term. It is like our school orchestra concert the other evening. When it ended, hundreds of chairs covered the gym. The conductor looked up into the balcony and asked for volunteers to put the chairs away. Scores of men, women, and youth grabbed the chairs, and the job was finished in minutes.

Classes concluding DISCIPLE: BECOMING DISCIPLES THROUGH BIBLE STUDY are amazed in Session 33 when they work to identify one another's spiritual gifts. Often people learn from others gifts they didn't know they had.

"You would be wonderful with the youth!"

"You really think so?"

"You would be a terrific leader for a new DISCIPLE group."

"Oh, I'm not a scholar."

"No, but you are a super facilitator."

"You have a warm, compassionate nature; you'd be great calling on the sick!"

Many DISCIPLE graduates, catching a vision of their gifts and of the call of Christ, have gone into the ministry. One seminary dean told me 20 to 30 percent of their incoming students mention DISCIPLE as an essential ingredient in their call. For the first time, they had struggled to identify their gifts.

Today's church requires:

- Everyone in ministry. You are a part of the body.
- Identification of gifts. We don't enjoy doing things we're not suited for.
- Everyone being put to work, assigned meaningful tasks, often short-term.
- Everyone being given adequate instruction, training, and supervision. The good news: Some are called to be "administrators." (Growing independent churches often hire lay staff to supervise this huge task of empowering the laity.)

My mom got sick when I was about thirteen. My sister, Beverly, was about six or seven. Dad was a busy funeral director with an emergency ambulance. A junior college girl lived with us to help answer the phone, keep an eye on us kids, and often help fix supper. With Mom in bed, Dad called us all together, and, in his most serious demeanor, said, "Gang, we're all going to have to pitch in. Everyone must help. Bev, you must set the table, pick up your clothes. Dick, you have to wash the dishes and vacuum the floor on Saturdays. All of us must check on Mom, and make sure she has what she needs."

That's the church today. It's crisis time. We're all going to have to pitch in.

Chapter 5 / BIGGER IS SMALLER

They had their meals together in their homes,

eating with glad and humble hearts, praising God . . .

And every day the Lord added to their group those who were being saved.

(Acts 2:46-47 GNT)

L ike a wind gusting across a Texas plain, a revival of religious interest is sweeping the American landscape. But like a barn with the doors locked tight or a farmhouse with the windows closed, the roaring wind scarcely penetrates most church structures.

Sociologists are trying to understand the upsurge of religious interest. For almost seventy years, "Gallup and other polling organizations have sought to gain insight into the *minds* and *hearts* of the populace, and, increasingly in recent years, the *souls* of Americans" (*Book Surveying the Religious Landscape,* George Gallup, Jr. and D. Michael Lindsay [Harrisburg, Penn.: Morehouse Publishing, 1999]). Their findings are dramatic. Over the last half century, the percentage of Americans who say they feel the need "to experience spiritual growth" has surged to over 80 percent (p. 1). Folks thinking about "the basic meaning and value of their lives" have jumped from half to over two-thirds of the population.

Yet, Gallup rightly asks: "Religion is broad, but is it deep?" (p. 3). Only about the same numbers of people are related to organized religion today as fifty years ago—about four in ten Americans report attending church "regularly." Gallup believes the spiritual wind is mostly blowing outside the church. He points to gaps—an ethics gap and a knowledge-of-the-Bible gap. He mentions the strange mixture of faith ideologies floating around in people's minds, like dry leaves drifting in the breeze. Many Americans, he argues, tend to view their faith as a matter between them and God and do not participate in any congregational life.

Examples of bewilderment abound. Ninety percent of adults say they pray regularly, yet half cannot name the first book in the Bible. Almost all (90 percent) want their children to receive religious training, yet fewer than half do.

Today the loneliness in our society coupled with "spiritual" interest is causing numbers of people to seek small-group participation, often in new, independent congregations, sometimes in non-church fellowships. "Small groups with religious interests are not a new phenomenon, but the current popularity of these gatherings is historically unprecedented" (p. 89). Surveyors of our culture like Robert Wuthnow, George Gallup, and George Barna certify that "both ecclesial and secular organizations are increasingly using small groups as a means to combat the fragmentation that occurs in today's society" (p. 90). The experts estimate that today's landscape reveals about 900,000 Bible study groups, 750,000 special-interest groups, and 500,000 self-help groups. Participants testify that they support one another emotionally, help one another feel closer to God, even give aid when some folks are sick or out of work.

Once we understood this in our historic churches. The German Pietist movement during the seventeenth century encouraged believers to meet together in "conventicles" or "colleges of piety"—small groups for spiritual growth and edification. The Wesley class meetings built on the experience of the Holy Club at Oxford. They met regularly for prayer, Bible study, and spiritual accountability. The Sunday school movement that swept across the prairies of America in the late 1800s relied on small classes led by lay teachers.

Would you be surprised if you discovered that growing congregations stress small group participation? Of course not. Not with dramatic examples like Saddleback Church in Los Angeles, Church of the Resurrection in Kansas City, Willow Creek near Chicago, and Mike Slaughter's Ginghamsburg church in Ohio. The tragedy is, so many churches stop, look, and listen, like cars stopped for a passing train, then continue on in their old travel patterns, still expecting new people to come into their old structures.

Consider Saddleback Church. In 1995, Rick Warren asked me,

along with many others, to read his manuscript for *The Purpose Driven Church.* I sensed immediately that this Baptist preacher in California understood today's secular America and was determined to launch his church with new strategies. Whereas my generation of preachers had focused on worship, pastoral care, church buildings, and organizational structure, Rick Warren focused on teaching, group life, spiritual growth, and almost cheerleaderlike missional encouragement. You might expect a California pastor to strip off his coat and necktie and go informal but, in the vast impersonal populations of Los Angeles, you would not anticipate his urgent stress on face-to-face relationships—nor his rather severe emphasis on learning the biblical walk, in stark contrast to the secular American lifestyle.

But I was not ready for the phenomenal acceptance of *The Purpose Driven Life,* which has now sold millions of copies. Our pastor son, Paul, during Lent, organized nearly fifty groups guided by that book. It seems like everybody is reading it. I walked into an airport and saw a salesman with a copy in his hand. I was not too surprised when, in 2005, I heard how Ashley Smith, an Atlanta woman taken hostage, helped calm her captor by reading from the book into the wee hours of the morning.

Rick Warren's gift of insight was to unite commitment and community from the get-go. He sensed early that what Gallup claims is true. People used to believe, then belong. Now, people have to belong before they believe! As a pastor, I am embarrassed how many people I received into church membership with a handshake and a prayer, then watched them drift away into inactivity. In the 1980s I began to urge all new members to join an adult Sunday school class, asking them, "Who will bring you soup when you're sick?" But pastors like Warren explain carefully to newcomers that face-to-face, committed, caring relationships are essential to believing and belonging. Those disciplines are required of individuals desiring to be disciples of Jesus. Warren built the culture of Saddleback on this belief: "The Bible knows nothing of solitary saints or spiritual hermits isolated from other believers and deprived of fellowship" (p. 130).

All Christians believe in "fellowship." But for many of us, the word has become watered down, as in "Stay after services for fellowship," or Sunday night will be a "fellowship dinner." The biblical word for fellowship is *koinonia,* which means "shared life together." Warren insists that his people experience life together. Then he bears down, "When it comes to fellowship, size matters: smaller is better. You can worship with a crowd but you can't fellowship with one. Once a group becomes larger than about ten people, someone stops participating" (pp. 138-39).

Why did the Wesley class meeting movement decline in the U.S.? Philip Hardt did an intensive study of early New York Methodism, particularly the class meeting (*The Soul of Methodism*). He documents the following: some leaders were dynamic, popular, knowledgeable. A pastor or a superb teacher would draw people into the group. Others, potential leaders, were intimidated. They felt inadequate and would demurely defer like a bashful boy at the school dance. The classes would grow in size. Twelve became twenty, twenty turned to thirty or forty. Then the group became stable, happy, satisfied, just like a modern adult Sunday school class. Unlike the original class meetings, these enlarged groups were not held accountable for training fresh leaders or initiating new groups. They didn't form new groups; the movement stopped in its tracks.

DISCIPLE churches often make two mistakes. Sometimes they enlarge a group that is led by the pastor or a popular teacher. As the size goes up, the spiritual impact goes down. But also, these churches fail to designate, train, and empower new leaders, new facilitators, so the movement fails to expand. Each class should develop two or three leaders who can launch new groups.

John Wesley had a vision of growth, expansion, multiplication, but it depended on keeping the classes small (living room size), constantly training new class leaders, and multiplying groups to include new potential converts. He insisted that the movement start small and grow, not with a larger group but with more groups and with a network of accountability. He made the group leaders attend a small leadership group to keep their method focused.

Charles Wesley understood that God starts small.

> When he first the work begun
> Small and feeble was his day
> Now the word doth swiftly run;
> Now it wins its widening way.

The Wesleys built on a biblical base. "For where two or three are gathered in my name, I am there among them" (Matt. 18:20). Like

DISCIPLE Bible study, they leaned on Acts 2:42, where the early Christians met in homes and "devoted themselves to the apostles' teaching and fellowship (*koinonia*), to the breaking of bread and the prayers." But small is not enough. For several years, my wife, Julia, and I led marriage therapy groups that met in our home each Wednesday night. These groups helped nearly half of the troubled marriages, about as many as professional therapists are able to help. (See *The Pastor and Marriage Therapy Groups* [Nashville: Abingdon, 1973].) Like our living room therapy groups, in the exploding, small group churches, fellowship means authenticity. "They share their hurts, reveal their feelings, confess their failures, disclose their doubts, admit their fears, acknowledge their weaknesses, and ask for help and prayer" (*The Purpose Driven Life,* Warren [Grand Rapids: Zondervan, 2002], p. 139). Compare this to Paul's admonition: "Share each other's troubles and problems, and in this way obey the law of Christ" (Gal 6:2 NLT).

However, our therapy groups lacked biblical focus, lacked Christ-centered acknowledgment. They needed a missional thrust to have really been Christian *koinonia*. Like many support groups of the 1970s and 1980s, including some of the "touchy-feelies," we were leery of too much Christianity.

In Kansas City, Pastor Adam Hamilton began his congregation in a funeral home, partly the inspiration for the name "Church of the Resurrection." Like Warren, he sensed the loneliness in society and the superficiality in many churches. He didn't want to end up with a 3,000-member church—one-third active, one-third dropping in occasionally, and one-third nowhere to be found. So, even now, with 9,000 in worship, he sits down on Sunday afternoons with people who declare interest in joining the church and tells them that they don't have to join—they can keep on visiting and have no responsibilities.

Then he gets serious. He tells them, in effect, but if you decide to stand before God and ask to be baptized or renew your baptism and take vows of church membership, here's what you will be doing. You will promise to worship weekly unless you are ill, even worshiping in a different town if you are traveling. You must begin a disciplined plan of giving. He tells them that he and his wife tithe, as the Bible mandates, and he hopes they will move quickly and carefully in that direction. He stresses that all of our members give time each year to at least one special mission project, so you will want to help with Habitat for

Humanity, a Volunteers in Mission project, the food pantry downtown, or teaching children, youth, or adults in our church school. Finally, you won't be happy in this church unless you are in a small Bible study group, regularly and consistently. We have DISCIPLE Bible study—almost everyone participates in that. We have Emmaus follow-up groups, or Alpha groups for fledgling Christians. Another option is Crown Ministries. Don't join this church unless you are ready to be in a face-to-face study of the Scriptures (*Leading Beyond the Walls* [Nashville: Abingdon, 2002]). I wish I had been that smart when I was a pastor.

This story comes out of Nashville: one morning a secretary in the DISCIPLE office of the United Methodist Publishing House answered the phone. She quickly put her hand over the speaker and spoke to a colleague, "I've got some kook on the phone—claims he wants $45,000 worth of DISCIPLE manuals."

Her colleague asked, "Who is it?"

"Someone from Kansas City, some church called Resurrection."

"Let me have it, let me have it," the supervisor shouted. "That's Adam Hamilton's church. They have over a thousand people a year in DISCIPLE!"

Sure enough, the church reached its goal of 1,000 people in DISCIPLE in 2000; now it's a normal pattern.

The point: Don't join the church unless you're serious. And don't just mutter words about being loyal with your prayers, your presence, your gifts, and your service. Be ready to be a Christian, regularly and intimately tied to others in the body of Christ.

If you study other growing churches, you will discover differences, but you will see heightened expectations (they have raised the bar) and a demand that people both belong and believe. An intimate church family will help keep members from backsliding. "Let us not give up the habit of meeting together, as some are doing. Instead, let us encourage one another" (Heb. 10:25 GNT).

Conflict

But notice! Each of the churches I've mentioned started from scratch, have had only one senior pastor across many years, and have developed a culture of high spiritual growth expectations, including small group life. Think how many existing churches have a different history, a contrasting way of thinking, a much different culture. Our son, Paul, finished his Doctor of Ministry degree by studying existing churches that were in decline, then were turned around and began to grow again. His findings are as frightening as a Kansas tornado on the horizon. Paul found, after studying many churches with 200-500 members that:

Turnaround did not occur unless there was some crisis. People were willing to stop and take stock.

The new pastor had a vision.

In adopting new approaches of outreach, in trying to make and teach new disciples, there was always conflict.

Mildly aware of the conflict, general church leaders, superintendents, and regional administrators were often distant and nonsupportive.

Those who start new congregations (may their tribe increase) can create a vibrant, high-expectation, small-group style. But pastors and church leaders who try to change the culture of an existing fellowship often face serious conflict. However, because a slow, lingering death of the congregation is the alternative, like a wrestler climbing into the ring, let's get into the fray. Remember, they excommunicated Martin Luther. They threw rocks and rotten tomatoes at John Wesley. When Jesus confronted the solidified religious structures of Judaism—trying to bring outsiders in—they crucified him.

Strategy

So how do we unravel a dying church culture? Here are some thoughts. First, as a local pastor and congregation, we remember—and discuss—whose we are and what we are called to do. We remember our Lord's post-resurrection instructions, his orders to "go out and train everyone you meet, far and near" (Matt. 28:19 *The Message*). Then we remember, sharing with one another, our own conversion experiences, our own commitment times, our own *yes* to Jesus. We talk about spiritual experiences. The old Wednesday night testimony meeting died out because a handful of saints told the same old faith stories over and over again. But now, fresh testimony is needed. Testimonies revitalize the memory and fuel the future. Our goal is a passion to make disciples.

We remember when people were won to the Lord, converted,

baptized, confirmed. Maybe my wife would tell about her dad's family in Arkansas, taking the milk cow to the ten-day camp meeting. Or we could talk about the energy and enthusiasm of revivals. Or when we sent lay persons—men mostly—out calling on neighborhood prospects in the 1950s and 1960s. Or recall aggressive youth camping when high-schoolers sat under a cross, contemplated life, and gave their hearts to Jesus. Or tell about a confirmation class culminating in a laying on of hands and a deep feeling of being right with God. Some might remember when lay people invited them to join a class or helped them put their children in Sunday school or invited them to eat at the pre-Lenten supper. The point: We can utilize the congregation's memories of becoming disciples, and we can build that memory into the emotional foundation for today's outreach efforts.

Some laity may recall when their congregation began years before. They might narrate how they canvassed the neighborhood, how the pastor went house to house, how they began new women's circles, a new men's group, a set of new adult Sunday school classes. Recently a young preacher, trying to energize his congregation, recalled the time long before when a beloved pastor had stepped out of the pulpit, took the keys to the church out of his pocket, and flung them out into the crowd. He cried out, "The doors of the church are open; the doors are open, all the time, to everybody. Let's invite them to come in."

With these emotion-fueled memories, new vision, new zeal for outreach strategy may fire up the disciple-making ministry—like cleaning the carburetor revitalizes an old car.

Now you're ready to talk strategy. That's where the rubber hits the road. One approach is to see DISCIPLE Bible study not as a treat for the saints, but as treatment for the world. Too many pastors lead a study or two, then let the program die. But when the church strategizes, sends the pastor and a layperson to training, develops a lay coordinator, allows graduates to give testimony, encourages facilitators to recruit, the study becomes a basis for outreach. (See DISCIPLE manual for particulars of how to build a movement, how to make DISCIPLE flourish in your church, your community. Note DVD available. Order from BeADisciple.com.)

When it comes to strategy for reaching people, some will want to try the old ways. Pastoral calling on the unchurched worked fifty years ago—people were impressed. Now they wonder why the pastor is calling on them. Two-by-two calling was powerful. Now the sign on the door (or the chain across the opening) says "No solicitors." Revivals in football stadiums only work for those who already love the Lord. Television worship is great for the deeply committed homebound, but it doesn't bring a wave of new converts into the fellowship.

I tried the "I Found It" campaign in Wichita. Lay folks made 5,000 telephone calls. Our evangelistic results were zero. One Roman Catholic, a problem drinker, promised to go talk to his priest. That is all the results we had. Like clothes out of style, efforts to help sinners find the Savior, help the lost and the lonely become part of the Christian fellowship must be appropriate for the times. Today's outreach must be lay-dominated, low-key, invitational, informal, small-group oriented—and each church will need to design and define its own unique strategy.

A neighborhood church in Little Rock was strong after World War II. Hardworking, middle-class folks bought modest homes and raised their children in the nearby church. But after thirty years, the children grew up and left home. Remaining members of the congregation were in their sixties and seventies. New young families were moving into those old neighborhood homes, but the church wasn't reaching them. The pastor, a gentle, loving man, was approaching retirement. Months in advance, the district superintendent asked the church leaders which they wanted in their new preacher—a kindly, older chaplain pastor or a young, energetic preacher who would change things to reach the neighborhood, like they had thirty years before.

Serious discussion took place. Finally, they voted to ask for an aggressive, disciple-making minister. One was appointed. He quickly found that, if a young family visited the church, there was no young adult class. So the family didn't return. The few young adult members already in place were scattered around, teaching Sunday school to children and youth. So the pastor went to the old-timers and said, "I want you folks to teach the children; I want the young adults to form a new class to welcome others."

The oldsters screamed to high heaven. "We've done that!" "We did that for twenty years, a lifetime ago." "We're too old."

The pastor cajoled, reminding them of their decision to grow. So they begrudgingly began to say, "Well, I'll teach for a year if you'll help me." "I'll work with the first and second graders, but just for a year." And the change was made, the door of invitation was thrown open, new adult classes were formed, and the church began to grow with new families. You should have heard the oldsters brag, two years later, about the children, the young families, the neighborhood people who were now in their church.

Wouldn't it be exciting if we obeyed Jesus' command to "go," "make disciples," "teaching them to obey everything that I have commanded" (Matt. 28:19-20)? And wouldn't it be fascinating if our best methodology was the New Testament style: Jesus teaching the Twelve, St. Paul clustering a group in prison, converts and inquirers meeting in one another's homes?

The gospel could explode in today's world with a handful of faithful believers at a time, even with a couple of doubters thrown in. We could overcome a famine of biblical ignorance and a desert of heart-wrenching loneliness with folks like you and me, who, in small group settings, "devoted themselves to the apostles' teaching and fellowship, to the breaking of bread and the prayers" (Acts 2:42)?

Chapter 6 / YOUTH

Let no one despise your youth, but set the believers an example in speech

and conduct, in love, in faith, in purity.

(1 Tim. 4:12)

When in retirement, I was sent as bishop in residence to Southwestern College in Winfield, Kansas, and I experienced cultural shock. Being thrown into the teen, young adult world—what George Gallup Jr. calls *millennials*—I felt like a bystander being flung, fully clothed, into a swimming pool.

I loved it. I had survived World War II crew cuts and Vietnam-era long hair. I danced to Dorsey's swing and Elvis's rock and roll. Now I see guys with tattoos and earrings, gals with two inches of waist showing above their blue jeans. Their jazz is loud and exuberant—they wiggle more than they dance. And I am immersed into a new technical environment of cell phones, laptops, Xboxes, iPods, and iPhones.

In one sense, kids are kids, no matter how they cut their hair or wear their clothes, no matter how loud the music or how they handle computer games and cell phones. Underneath the trendy fad trappings, they are still the young human beings with all the thoughts and emotions, all the pent-up energy and confused aspirations that youth have always had.

But in another sense, times do change, social life and church life change. Attitudes toward authority, the Bible, and the church bend and reshape. George Gallup, Jr., after a mountain of research, describes the signs of the times (*The Gallup Guide: Reality Check for*

21st Century Churches [Loveland, Colo.: Group Publishing, 2002], p. 5). Gallup insists that teens today "show these qualities: idealism, optimism, spontaneity, and exuberance. . . . They are enthusiastic about helping others. . . . They want clear rules to live by; they want clarity" (p. 15). Teens, like most Americans, believe that life is meaningful and has a purpose. Yet as many as two-thirds believe "that most churches and synagogues today are not effective in helping people find meaning in life" (p. 13). They are well aware of the world they live in. They have witnessed (experienced) 9/11, war with Iraq, and a tsunami. They know, sometimes firsthand, the downside of America: "child pornography, high levels of crime and gun deaths, widespread child and spouse abuse, alcohol and drug abuse, fatherlessness, and the lack of a sexual ethic. They know, in spades, that every other marriage today will break up, spreading dysfunction throughout society" (p. 9).

Today's pressures are immense. I asked Lindsay Morgan, a twenty-year-old college junior, "What about pressure?"

"Kids today are under pressure to excel. They start playing ball at age five, play on a winter team, travel the U.S. on a competitive summer team, and are expected to join the National Basketball Association by the time they finish high school. Colleges demand above-average test scores to land scholarships. Jobs are competitive, often requiring early work experiences before even being hired. The question always asked is 'Who's Number One?' " she replies.

"The other pressure is technological," she continues. "I can sit at my desk, turn on my laptop, and research from the Library of Congress. My roommate has her iPod on, listening to music; we're recording a TV movie on our TIVO. I need to get my car serviced. There is a jazz concert at 7 p.m. No wonder George Barna says we kids 'sadly are likely to gain the reputation for being the most information-overloaded group ever.' We have too much data. Too much pressure."

My experience with college students reveals an eagerness to understand things spiritual, coupled with a disinterest in denominational labels. Students are eager to volunteer to build Habitat for Humanity houses; to travel to Juarez, Mexico, on a work team; or to repair homes of the elderly in our community. They don't care whether the event is sponsored by the Baptists, the Catholics, or the Fellowship of Christian Athletes. One problem, call it a dilemma, for the church is this: they are suspicious (or at least unimpressed) by authority and, at the same time, eager for clarity, for specific, clear, understandable guidelines. I think they would say they want the guidelines, the beliefs, the rules clearly expressed. Then they want the freedom to buy in or walk away.

We began to feel the shift away from traditional upbringing and rather nonanalytical acceptance as early as the late 1960s. Students would go from churches in Kansas towns to Kansas State University, and Campus Crusaders would say to them during the first week on campus: "Are you saved?"

They would respond, "Well, I grew up in the Presbyterian Church," or "I've gone to Sunday school all my life and I belong to the Methodist Church."

"But are you saved? Have you been forgiven of your sins and do you know Jesus Christ as your personal Lord and Savior? Here, sit down and I will explain to you, from scripture, the four spiritual laws." The clarity, the specific encounter with another student, the deep spirituality of it all, appealed to many—many who, if asked earlier what they believed, would be fuzzy and unclear.

Years later, in the late 1980s, when I was chair of the Church Growth Committee of the Council of Bishops of The United Methodist Church, I talked to several Campus Crusade professional leaders. "Is it still working," I asked, "the face-to-face encounter with the four spiritual laws?"

"Oh, no," they responded. "Students are suspicious. They don't trust anybody on first encounter anymore. They want to bite the nickel to see if it's real."

"So, what do you do?" I asked. "Why, we invite them to a small group Bible study where we listen to their inner feelings, and share and study and pray—and hope to eventually lead them into a deep faith commitment."

Then one of them, a Baptist, laughed at me and said, "We're rediscovering the Wesley class meeting!"

Relationships

I've read what the experts say about contemporary youth culture. But I wanted to know more firsthand. So I asked Natalie Carlson, age twenty-one: "What's it like? What do young people want and need in the church?" I was expecting to hear about guitars and trap drums, about people standing, raising their arms, and clapping. And I anticipated stories about mission trips to Guatemala or to the inner city of Philadelphia.

Instead, Natalie exclaimed, "The one basic thing all youth are searching for is relationships! Think about complaints against youth today—drugs, sex, alcohol, gangs. Why do youth fill their lives with these experiences? Because they are empty. If you ask youth today what is their number one struggle, they'll answer 'loneliness.' We want relationships, not only with God, but also with people."

Then, Natalie started preaching: "Older adults are looking for quick fixes to get youth into churches. A few people pour hours into programming events. Others give money. But we don't want their money. We want them. We want their time. We want to know them and to have them know and love us. Let us help make the plans with them and carry out the plans with them."

"What about Jesus Christ and moral behaviors?" I asked.

"These aren't new problems," Natalie answered. "Youth are trying to fill a deeper longing, just like people did in the Scriptures. Help us form personal friendships with Christians and help us develop a personal relationship with Christ. Youth, as they follow God's way on an intimate level, will quickly realize that 'immoral' things are no longer needed. Also, within a caring fellowship, the issue of morals can be thoughtfully addressed."

Natalie pointed out how few young women have a "mentor"—a spiritual relationship with an older Christian woman. "The issue," she said, "is time. Do they have time for us?"

Recently, Natalie organized a conference on the Southwestern campus for women, young and old, called "Treasured Connections." Sixty women came from over fifteen churches. They talked about hobbies such as gardening, fashion, cooking, and fitness across the age lines. They even discussed mentoring—yoking a youth with an older Christian woman, meeting together once a week.

I reflected on George Barna's study in 2001 that found that "only 34 percent of Baby Busters (ages 18-35) say they are absolutely committed to the Christian faith; compared to 52 percent of Baby Boomers (ages 36-54), 63 percent of the Builders (ages 55-73), and 70 percent of the Seniors (ages 74 and older)" ("Annual Study

Reveals America Is Spiritually Stagnant" by The Barna Group, http://www.barna.org/FlexPage.aspx?Page=BarnaUpdate&BarnaUp dateID=84 [accessed August 2007]).

I've been arguing that youth and young adults want participation, involvement, action. Natalie agrees, but insists that youth are looking for "acceptance, connection, relationship, and relevance. Youth often feel underappreciated. We want to be a part of the team, a participant in helping plan and develop things."

She quotes Barna, "Many young people feel overlooked as potential leaders." And they want additional training to do it.

Leadership

I decided to ask Lindsay another question: "What are young people searching for today?"

"Young people want to lead!" she exclaimed. "Youth are exuberant, passionate, and ready to take the world head on. They possess energy and creativity. They harness hope. They flourish in new possibilities."

She continued with a story about two young women at her college. "They were unsatisfied with the wastefulness on campus. Plastic bottles, newspapers, aluminum cans, and glass were all shoved into regular trash bins and transported to the city dump. The girls wondered why a small college campus was not just as capable of fighting for the environment as big universities and cities. So instead of giving into red-tape demands or slumping back into helplessness, the girls initiated the first-ever recycling program on campus. Three years later, recycling bins can be found in every building, including the dormitories, and the college boasts to visitors about its very own recycling shed. Youth can bring this same creativity and inventiveness to the church, but they have to first be given the chance."

Author Kenda Creasy Dean claims that the church currently fails to provide this chance. "On the whole," she writes, "mainline denominations have overlooked youth as a mission field—thinking of it instead as a program, a subsidiary point of involvement in the church life.... There is nothing ultimate in committing to a youth fellowship group ... [and] we do not encourage serious commitment from youth when we talk about activities and programs" (*Practicing*

Passion: Youth and the Quest for a Passionate Church [Grand Rapids: William B. Eerdmans, 2004], pp. 3-7).

Natalie says, "Pizza parties, car washes, and Wednesday night games are all wonderful, but aren't youth capable of a whole lot more? I believe so, and so do others my age. Youth programs need to focus less on entertaining the young and more on allowing them to create opportunities to share the powerful message of Christ."

Adam Wilbur, a sophomore at a Christian church in Wichita, Kansas, calls it ownership. "We want to actually have a say in what our youth group does. We want to decide how it should affect people," he explains. "Whether it's through a special student leadership group, youth that help lead worship services, or some other radical idea, youth have to be given the chance to lead ... or they'll leave."

Have you studied the living room church movement? *Time* magazine claims that several thousand youth and young adults have turned their backs on buildings and pulpits and denominations. They are going to a home with a dish of food, a Bible, and maybe a guitar. For the next two to four hours they sing praises, share spiritual and emotional needs, eat supper, read scripture, give testimony, give and receive the bread and the chalice. "It *is* the service. There is no pastor, choir, or sermon" (*Time* 3/6/06, p. 47).

Maybe this movement won't sweep away the denominations as George Barna predicts (*Revolution* [Carol Stream, Ill.: Tyndale House, 2005]). But it does show that young people want a piece of the action. And it underlines the words of Jesus: "Where two or three are gathered together in my name, I am there among them" (Matt. 18:20).

The Cultural Gap in Worship

Before we discuss trap drums and acoustical guitars, let's look at youth worship as a whole. Old-timers who simply roll their eyes and clamp their hands over their ears at praise music are not digging deep enough. The revolution is profound. I wish we old-timers were *older*. I wish we could remember the Wesleyan movement in England when we were called the Shouting Methodists, when Charles Wesley grabbed popular tunes and made hymns out of them. I wish we could recall the 1880s when Wesleyans, holiness folks, and others went to camp meetings and preached and prayed and sang and clapped. I wish we could even recall revivals when the piano crashed out "We're Marching to Zion" and "Washed in the Blood," when people wept, when men and women knelt at prayer rails, when the Holy Spirit swept over the crowd, when people were saved. When did we become sedate, solemn, and sophisticated? When did the educated preacher, the pipe organ, and the robed choir produce a quiet congregation sitting on their hands and listening? When did people put on suits and best dresses to go to church? Was it after poor, hardworking shopkeepers and farmers did Methodist things like abstaining from alcohol and gambling, saving their money, going to college, and becoming upper-middle-class? In any event, kids today want action. They want to participate. They want emotion.

Participation

When I studied algebra, I took notes, studied my textbook, and got ready for the test—quietly and alone. Today's kids work in teams, ask questions, sit around circular tables, dialogue on the Internet, share their findings. Or instead of studying Spanish out of a book—or even merely listening to bilingual records—they go with a group to Mexico or Spain. It's hands-on, working and talking together—participation. Come to our Wednesday voluntary morning worship at the college. We don't have a chapel building. We have no stained glass, no pulpit, just a large room full of students (and a few faculty and staff). Everyone is standing up clapping as the praise band and miked singers lead us in twenty minutes of song. I have learned to use my arms to bring Christ down, put him on the cross, bury him in the tomb, and raise him in glory as we sing: "Lord, I Lift Your Name on High." Come prayer time, a student leader asks for needs and concerns. A sophomore girl speaks softly, unable to hold back the tears, and says her mother is dying of cancer. Everyone joins hands and prays silently or aloud for Mom. A guy is pleading that he has a friend on drugs and will ask that we all get down on our knees and pray for him. Episcopalians and Pentecostals, Baptists and United Methodists are all in prayer. One day, the theme was forgetting past mistakes, so the student leader passed out a piece of blank paper to everyone. We wrote our griefs, our mistakes, our sins, on the paper, then brought the notes forward to throw them into a fiery cauldron of divine forgiveness.

A student reads the scripture. The passage is challenging, relevant, projected on the screen so that everyone can join in. The message, usually given by a guest speaker, is honest, straightforward, to the point. The clear demand is part of the appeal.

At announcement time, a student reminds those interested of an 11 p.m. Bible study Thursday night. Another student tells about a Fellowship of Christian Athletes rally. Don't forget the Christian rock concert in a nearby city. Oh yes, a volunteer work team is going to Wichita Saturday to help distribute food in the Urban Ministry Food Pantry. The World Witness Team is conducting services in a distant town next week, and the Keynotes are singing next Sunday at a nearby church. It's a busy fifty-five minutes, but it's an exciting, invigorating, student-led, Christ-centered, participatory event.

Feelings

Let's talk about emotion. Feelings. Everyone has feelings, but not everyone expresses them—and not in the same way. Not in the same places. Not in church. The same somber deacon who sits quiet as a church mouse while the pastor preaches may jump up and down screaming at the high school basketball game. When is it okay to feel and to express feelings in church?

I am a white male, German descendant, a thinker—not a feeler—on the Myers-Briggs personality profile. My father, a nonemotional funeral director, influenced me; the tight-lipped cowboys like John Wayne guided my youthful outward expression. But across the years, I have been privileged to worship with a rich variety of Christians around the world: black Pentecostals from 8 p.m. until midnight, Roman Catholics at daily mass, Costa Rican Methodists who clap and sing. The Methodist churches in Cuba and Brazil came alive and reached great numbers of new people when they became more "charismatic." (Charismatic today often means enthusiastic, emotionally and physically expressive.)

In traditional, United States mainline worship, we're faced with a radical shift in culture. Forget the piercings and tattoos. Think feelings. Youth think we somber oldsters are hiding the truth when we cloister our emotions. Expression of feelings means it's okay to cry in church if your heart is breaking, good to raise your hands in praise when you are drawn God-ward, helpful to hug a neighbor to show love and acceptance. Remember the old ditty, "If you're happy and you know it clap your hands"? Kids today want to be open, authentic, expressive, even exuberant with their emotions in church.

Music

Now back to trap drums and electronic guitars. No question that the music revolution is fully on us. I love Bach's "Jesu, Joy of Man's Desiring" on the pipe organ, but Saddleback, Church of the Resurrection, and Willow Creek don't have pipe organs. In college chapel we don't even use a piano. Keyboard, drums, acoustical guitars, and student voices help us sing the praise songs. I'm an old percussionist, so I can handle the beat, but some of my friends roll their eyes. Criticism comes from all quarters. Youth want the music of their lives to flow into their worship.

I asked Lindsay what it's like becoming a young adult in the twenty-first century.

She replied, "I agree with the researchers who say my generation is experiencing the greatest wake of change." She claims that the evidence is overwhelming: "Social customs have changed radically—even in the past five years."

Suppose you were going to be a missionary to Bolivia—say, up high on the altiplano. You would learn Spanish, of course, but you would also learn the native Almira. You would eat potatoes and listen to the local music. You would immerse yourself in the local culture so that you could convey the gospel in the people's idiom.

Today's youth don't want merely to listen to a choir; they want to sing. And they want to sing the song again and again. Then sing another song and clap, and smile and rock and wiggle. They want to hear instruments that they know and love—instruments that have been stirring their thoughts and emotions for over a quarter of a century—acoustical instruments, guitars and banjos, trap drums and keyboard. And it's OK to add a sax or a violin or a clarinet or two. You can talk about the Beatles or Elvis or 50 Cent or Justin Timberlake—but the music revolution has occurred, and, just as a missionary works within a culture, so the church of Jesus Christ must enter into this musical context. That's why congreation after congregation is developing alternative worship, contemporary services, blended worship, and the like. If we love our youth and want them to love and worship the Lord, we must understand and enter into their culture. We may find ways to comfort the older generation, but we are admonished to "go ... and make disciples of all nations" (Matt. 28:18 RSV), and that means going into the world of today's young people!

Two Paths

"Years ago," Lindsay noted, "Mom said it was a rarity for couples to move in together before they were married. Today I know six different college couples who live together. Growing up, a third of my peers came from a split home; today, it seems like nearly everybody's folks are divorced. Ethical absolutes are out the window. So much is considered 'acceptable.' Last week I went to my girls' soccer team practice. Teammates talked about upcoming parties, about how they 'couldn't wait to get wasted.' They joked about times they had passed out in one another's houses and had 'made out' with random guys. As I went back to my dorm, hot and sweaty from practice, I hit a wall of smoke. Two guys were puffing outside the dorm door, one with a cigarette and one with a marijuana joint."

Our youth culture today, as far as Christian faith is concerned, is "oil and water." That is, young people must decide which way to go—the secular way or the Jesus way. Everybody believes in God. Most people think they can do whatever they want to. But those youth who give their hearts to Jesus Christ know that they must walk a different path. Do you remember Robert Frost's words?

> Two roads diverged in a wood, and I—
> I took the one less traveled by
> And that has made all the difference.

That's the way youth feel. The path is narrow, sometimes lonely, daily in contrast, even in tension, with the path many young people are walking. Serious-minded, Christ-centered youth today often don't get much help from the church. They crave the scriptures, hungering for the words of Jesus to sustain them against societal seductions. They desperately need our Lord's assurance that "Everyone ... who hears these words of mine and acts on them will be like a wise man who built his house on rock" (Matt. 7:24).

Experts say churches that fail to attract young people talk more about God as Creator, Father. Churches that draw youth emphasize Jesus and the Holy Spirit. Kids are looking for "the way" and for the power to walk it. In a world of generalities, a world where everybody "believes in God," a world of a thousand opinions, youth crave clarity, concreteness. They find specificity in the incarnation. They hear the call of salvation, of discipleship, in Jesus. They experience inner feelings and sustenance from the Holy Spirit.

And youth are willing to be mentored. St. Paul nurtured Timothy, practically from childhood. He included him, taught him, developed his leadership gifts and graces. Here's how *The Message* recalls Paul's counsel to Timothy: "Don't let anyone put you down because you're young. Teach believers with your life: by word, by demeanor, by love, by faith, by integrity" (1 Tim. 4:12).

Your Future

But an even deeper need permeates the young Christian mind. "Why are you old-timers so focused on daily life choices?" asked Lindsay. "That's the easy part. Once we've accepted the Lord as our Savior, once we've found some Christian friends, once we've watched others think they're having fun and then crash and burn, we celebrate the Way. Most of the time. We believe Jesus is not 'yes and no,' but 'yes.'

"But the big concern, what am I going to do for Him and with Him in the future, is tough. The world's in a gigantic mess; what can we do to help?"

Lindsay says, "Hardly a day passes that I don't ponder my future. I often feel I have been given a giant vessel to sail wherever I please. The vessel comes complete with a crew (my safety net of family and friends). It is stocked with provisions (Christian nurturing, good health, higher education.) My ship's sails are squared into the wind of opportunity. For me, and for many youth and young adults, the question is: 'Where am I supposed to sail my ship?' "

Lindsay's comments helped me remember when a fourteen-year-old boy came up to me after church and told me that God wanted him to be a medical missionary. I was hesitant to encourage a boy so young. I told him to pray and follow the Lord's leading. I saw him a few weeks ago. He has completed eighteen years as a medical missionary.

I recall when I was seventeen. My best friend and I went to Cleveland, Ohio, for a massive youth conference. Richard Raines, later to become Bishop Raines, laid it on us. He said the *needs* of the world are like a *horizontal* bar: all sorts of needs—spiritual, physical, social—are sprinkled across it. People need food and shoes and instruction and faith. But our individual gifts and graces are unique. These God-given abilities are the **vertical** bar. Where those two beams intersect, the needs of the world (horizontal) and individual gifts (vertical), a cross is formed. God's call is at the center of that cross. My friend felt called to be a doctor. I felt called to be a preacher. Christian young people need to hear that message.

Also, the church can help kids experience the pain in the world. They want participation: let them participate. An eighteen-year-old told me about working one summer in the inner city of Philadelphia. She said the faces of the children are still in her mind's eye. A high schooler just got back from New Orleans. "It wasn't just fixing houses," he said. "It was talking with the people." An Assembly of God preacher thanked him profusely for coming, then told him as they stood in rubble, that God was going to bring good out of tragedy.

Wake up, church. Let young people lead the singing, give testimony, go with elders on work teams. Let them help plan retreats and vacation Bible schools. Permit high schoolers to take DISCIPLE, let college students lead study and prayer groups. Take them to church camps and revivals "where the action is." Let them give their hearts to Jesus and be disciples—now! Their ears and eyes are open for "the call."

I've always admired the Mormons for challenging young people to give two years to their church. Sometimes, I visit with them when they come to our door. (Sometimes I ask them why they don't drink coffee or smoke cigarettes.) Think what might happen if we thrust more of our youth into significant leadership roles—calling on the unchurched, teaching small children, playing guitar in the praise band.

Our granddaughter, Katie, called us from Senegal, Africa, on her cell phone. She serves as a Peace Corps volunteer. She is assigned to a tiny village to do ministry and medical care for mothers and small children. She says it is hot, over 120 degrees. She has her own hut, her own latrine, her own mosquito net, her own water. Wow! Isn't it amazing what young people can do when they feel called into service? "Let no one despise your youth" (1 Tim. 4:12).

Chapter 7 / CHILDREN

Let the little children come to me, and do not stop them;

for it is to such as these that the kingdom of God belongs.

(Luke 18:16)

I drove hard one afternoon in Arkansas, trying desperately to arrive at a local church meeting on time. Just when I hit town, I entered a school zone. School was letting out, and before I knew it, I was inching my way along, surrounded by happy kids who were laughing and ambling across the street. I drove slowly, frustrated as a fellow standing in a long line at a fast food joint.

Later, at the church meeting, I met with the congregational leaders—folks over forty, most over sixty, like me. We studied the decline of their Sunday school. They corporately complained about the general decline in worship. I raised the issue of children—they had so few in Sunday school, in confirmation, in the youth program. Then one old-timer hit me right between the eyes: "Oh, we don't have any kids anymore. They've all grown up and mostly moved away." I couldn't help it. I blurted out my afternoon experience a few blocks from the church when I had to stop and creep along to avoid hitting a boy or girl in a throng of children. Then came the knife-in-my-heart rejoinder, "Oh, those aren't *our* kids," he said. I wept inside, remembering the disciples who didn't want to be bothered by the wiggling, talkative children of others. It was as if they had said, "These children are not our children; send them away!"

Jesus' rebuff was quite stern. "Let the little children come to me," he said, "for it is to such as these that the kingdom of God belongs"

(Luke 18:16). Then he literally took children in his arms and blessed them.

Do you remember why the Sunday school began in John Wesley's England? Why "school"? Because they were not in school. Why Sunday? Because they were working, on the farms, in the village workplaces, even in the mines—as young as five years of age; laboring six days a week; eight, ten, twelve hours a day. Sunday was the only window of opportunity.

Why the Bible? Because it was about the only book they could get their hands on (books were scarce) and because the Wesleyans wanted to teach the kids—all the kids they could reach—about Jesus Christ and his loving, saving ways.

Wesleyans of all persuasions and Baptists of all varieties swept the American frontier with Sunday schools. They reached out to all the children of the region. At the turn of the twentieth century, there were twice as many people in Methodist Sunday schools on Sunday mornings as there were members of the congregations. Try that statistic on for size in your congregation!

As late as the 1950s, the head of the FBI, J. Edgar Hoover, noted the size, the strength, the spiritual impact of this ministry with children when he commented publicly, "Our jails are not full of graduates of Methodist Sunday schools."

We have more children in America today than ever before. But they are not *our* children. Our United Methodist denomination, like others, is getting older. The average Methodist is about six to eight years older than the national adult average. Some people wonder why membership rolls are in decline. The answer is not that people are racing to other churches, membership papers in hand, ready to transfer. No, not at all: more people transfer in than transfer out. The answer is, people are getting old, they are dying, going to heaven. They are transferring to the church triumphant, leaving empty pews behind, and there is no one to take their place.

How to Reach Children

Belatedly, but significantly, creative churches are designing bold new strategies to reach kids for the Lord. (Remember: 85 percent of church members make their Christ-centered commitment before age eighteen.) In churches developing contemporary worship or simply having three or four (or six) worship services, multiple Sunday schools are designed. The task is tough and slow in developing. The old rural (farm) mentality—take a bath on Saturday night, do the milking early Sunday morning, put the pot roast in the oven, take the whole family to 9:30 a.m. Sunday school and 11:00 a.m. worship—is slow to die.

In a 24/7 world, with people working all hours of the day and night, and in a revolutionary worship culture where some want Bach on the pipe organ and others want praise music with trap drums and guitars, multiple worship services are a must in many churches. But many a church starts by designing worship hours and forgets the Sunday school!

Add a 9:30 a.m. contemporary worship without careful planning, and soon the small children will be in Sunday school, never to be in worship; and the older children, youth, and adults will be in worship, never to be in Sunday school. Membership will rise, Sunday school will decline. People start thinking one hour at the church. A pastor in Texas said not one youth in her confirmation class had ever attended a worship service, and none of their parents were in an adult Sunday school class! In some churches, as soon as the children quit wiggling, they worship with their parents, on occasion, and don't go to Sunday school at all!

On the plus side, First United Methodist Church in Lawrenceville, a suburb of Atlanta, Georgia, strategized for Christian education as they struggled with worship. Sunday school at 8:30, 9:30, and 11:00 a.m. are all carefully encouraged, with classes for all ages at each hour. The task requires organization—choirs, ushers, teachers—but if the underlying assumption is strong (everyone is a student in the church school, and the times must fit both study and worship), then a plan must be devised.

New Approaches

I walked into First United Methodist Church right in the heart of downtown Little Rock, Arkansas, and the pastor's eyes were all aglow. "Come with me," she said. "We've doubled our Sunday school." As I walked through the old hallways, I saw fresh murals on the walls. The rooms were redecorated, reorganized. "It's called 'ROTATION,'" she said. "With professionals and lay helpers, we've developed a whole new style of Christian education—different ways of learning, different rooms for different styles of teaching." She even claimed they had to start a new adult class for parents because the children were so excited about coming on Sunday. "Of course, it required three times as many teachers," she said, "but only for a month at a time—and they love it!"

I asked my young college friend, Lindsay Morgan, to visit the rotational Sunday school at St. Luke's United Methodist Church in Oklahoma City. When she returned, she wrote:

"The scent of buttery popcorn filled my nostrils as I stepped into the dark entrance of Pyramid Pictures at St. Luke's United Methodist Church. All around me children sat on church pew benches swinging their feet and stuffing fistfuls of popcorn into their mouths. Their eyes gaped at a movie screen showing *Moses and the Ten Commandments*. A little girl watched the dancing Israelites and grew wide-eyed as Moses wrathfully raised the two stone tablets above his head. I chuckled at the girl and allowed my eyes to wander around the room. Beautiful velvet curtains lined the projector screen. Long, golden frames that depicted scenes of Jesus' life festooned the walls around me. For a brief moment, I forgot that I was visiting a church Sunday school and allowed myself to simply go to the movies.

"What an experience! What a Sunday school classroom! I had seen high-tech Sunday school classrooms before, full of blinking cosmic lights and gleaming flatscreen TVs. But this was different. It was teaching the Bible to children in a new way."

Lindsay reported, "The Pyramid Pictures movie theater is one of nine specially designed classrooms in St. Luke's Great Adventure Rotational Sunday School. The rooms, which house rotations of children in kindergarten through fifth grade for two services every Sunday, are packed with opportunities to exhibit creativity. The Jungle Jammin' room, for example, is filled with sounds of clapping and laughter as kids sing karaoke and dance to drumbeats. Glow-in-the-dark stars line the hallway to the Cyber Room and prepare children for deep-space adventures on computer software. Paris Plaza contains patio tables where students cook desserts and construct crafts relating to a Bible topic. And there are many more: the Mountain Movers game room, the King's Court theater stage, the Good News Network TV recording studio, the Jordan's Journey storytelling center, and the Boom Town science experiment lab. Each simultaneously utilizes the resources of the church and provides a fun learning environment for children.

"All the rooms exist as part of a new framework entitled Rotational Sunday School. Beginning in the early 1990s, this rotational model was designed by Presbyterian churches in the Chicago suburbs to combat boring Bible lessons, boring Sunday school activities, and bored children.

"Charlotte Teel, director of St. Luke's Children's Ministries, found out about the model when she was encouraged by the Reverend Bob Long, senior pastor, to visit a Fort Worth United Methodist Church in January 2001. Charlotte studied Fort Worth's model and returned ready to put her own ideas into action at St. Luke's.

"The rotation model centers upon the concept of selecting a single Bible story for an entire month," Lindsay continued. "For example, several months ago, St. Luke's focused upon the story of Noah's ark. Children were divided by grade level and assigned a different room for each week. Second graders traveled to the Jungle Jammin' room during week one to rattle a chorus of rain sticks. Why rain sticks? Because God flooded the earth with rain. During week two, the second graders shuttled to the Mountain Movers game room where they went on a scavenger hunt for different colors of yarn to make a rainbow necklace that would remind them of God's promise after the flood. Finally, in Paris Plaza, during week three, the second graders used cookie cutters to create animal shapes out of flour tortillas and make delicious plates of ark animal nachos." Lindsay's report blew my mind.

Have you read *7 Kinds of Smart* by Thomas Armstrong? He teaches multiple intelligence theory at the University of California. Some people learn verbally, some through pictures, others by bodily action or in music. Still others calculate mathematically, or learn in social settings or by meditating alone. The church has played with these ideas across the years with songs and crayons, but now comes a mighty, crash-through innovation.

Until recently, I thought education meant reading books, listening to a teacher, watching spelling words and algebraic equations scribbled on a blackboard, taking tests and writing term papers. But now, students—and people of all ages—are learning by doing, often in a variety of ways. At Southwestern College, Winfield, Kansas, the leadership team is learning organizational skills by guiding a freshman workday or building work teams. Student nurses help in care homes and in facilities for the developmentally disabled. A cluster of chemistry students struggle together with a lab experiment. Composition students critique their papers with PowerPoint presentations.

"Different children learn in different ways, and the rotational Sunday school model is designed to accommodate this fact," Lindsay notes. "The model is based upon the concept of multiple intelligences presented by author and Harvard professor Howard Gardner. In his book *Frames of Mind: The Theory of Multiple Intelligences,* Gardner reveals that at least seven different intelligences exist in the world today. He believes that if children are given a chance to exercise their specific intelligences at a young age, they have a better chance of learning information ([New York: Perseus Books, 1993], p. 10). This is exactly what the rotational Sunday school model strives to do."

Charlotte Teel of St. Luke United Methodist Church, Oklahoma City, declares that one of the major problems with conventional Sunday school is low retention of information. "We remember only 10 percent of what we read, 20 percent of what we hear, 30 percent of what we see ... (but) 100 percent of what we experience," she explains. Sunday school at St. Luke's is all about experience. Children with high musical intelligence are invited to demonstrate their sensitivity to melody, rhythm, and tone in the Jungle Jammin' room. Kids who possess logical-mathematical intelligence are asked to display it by performing measuring experiments in the Boom Town room. Repeat the same story in several different formats, and more kids will learn.

"The rotational model appears to be better for teachers as well," Lindsay continues. "Instead of teaching year-round, teachers are only needed for a single month to teach a single lesson. A different small group comes to that room each Sunday. Teachers are selected based upon their specific talents. So, if a young man is a skilled basketball player, he can elect to teach the lesson in the Mountain Movers game room where kids are expected to run and play—his forte—for a whole month (a "mentor" or adult "friend" travels with them week by week, but doesn't have to teach).

"Before rotational Sunday school, the St. Luke's children's program had plummeted to an all-time low of three elementary classes, six teachers, and thirty children. Like a beached whale washed ashore and gasping for a watery breath, the program was on the verge of death. However, with the implementation of the Great Adventure model, the church has experienced a major turnaround. Children's Sunday school attendance climbed from 80 children in 2000 to 165 after the 2001 reopening—a 106 percent increase in attendance! The statistics have continued to mount. In 2004, attendance for the Great Adventure was at 216 children, a 30 percent increase from 2001. Now the nine different classrooms are guided by some 40-50 staff members and volunteers annually.

"The enthusiasm that St. Luke's members are beginning to feel about the rotational Sunday school program is gradually spreading. A construction project to remodel a wing of the church into a Wee Adventure Sunday School program for children under the age of kindergarten is currently underway. Also, the Great Adventure Rotational Sunday School curriculum is now available to the world through a website called www.Rotation.org. Exactly how to engage children in Sunday school has been an issue in churches for almost twenty years. Now churches are beginning to share the methods that work.

"The fact that the rotational model of Sunday school can be shared is perhaps the most beautiful feature about it. Any church—or anyone for that matter—willing to follow the vision, can implement the program. Sure, some churches may enhance their program with fancy stages and high-tech gadgets. But others may simply use a bit of paint and some creative managing of resources to revitalize their curriculum.

"The rotational Sunday school program does not have to be fancy to work. The success of the program rests in the fact that the Word of God is being taught to children in different ways. The message has not changed from that of conventional Sunday school, but the delivery format has," Lindsay concludes.

LIVE B.I.G.

The United Methodist Publishing House (Cokesbury) launched a wildly new and different approach to Sunday school in 2006.

Responding in part to the successful rotational Sunday school and fully aware of dramatic changes in the way children learn today, Cokesbury produced LIVE B.I.G. for children three to thirteen. This material is no mere tweak of regular Sunday school curriculum; rather, it is, in church circles, revolutionary.

DVDs for ages three to four and five to six, for instance, feature Backyard Time set in Mr. Z's backyard. With Ms. Lucy as cohost and help from Bongo the Bible Bird, children laugh, hear Bible stories, and learn Bible verses, even at a very young age. Picture Time illustrates the Bible story with art, photos, and videos. Travel Time takes the children visually on trips to other churches and missions where Christians are living out their faith in Christ. The B.I.G. Sound, for ages seven to eight and nine to ten, includes songs and hymns and one original song per month, performed by a costumed cast who move and sing with zeal. The songs even include sign language. Tweens, ages eleven to thirteen, gather in the Common Ground Café where they discuss the life situations they face. Will, the soft-spoken host, is proprietor of the café, assisted by teen role models C.J., Julia, Kate, and Micah. In The B.I.G. Sound, tweens will sing along with contemporary Christian artists such as the Newsboys, Casting Crowns, and Rachel Lampa.

The material takes special care to be racially and gender inclusive. Teachers are aided with simplified lesson plans, a DVD section each week, and fun learning activities. A special curriculum aids the small church that has to put all their children in one class—called One B.I.G. Room.

Eric Strader directs youth ministries at College Hill United Methodist Church in Wichita, Kansas. After studying LIVE B.I.G. during the summer of 2006, he began using it in the fall, almost as soon as it was available, with middle-school girls—sixth and seventh graders. "I love the multimedia," he exclaims, "the mime movies, the music videos!" He has about a dozen tweens who respond vigorously to Bible stories built into numerous multisensory activities. One week they're acting, another they're cooking or drawing or singing. He uses three teachers in an informal rotation. They keep in touch regularly and one or two are present each Sunday.

"Our kids get nearly a full hour. They need the visual approach to help the Scriptures make more sense! Now when folks say Noah, or rainbow, or flood, the kids know what they're talking about. They are growing in their understanding of the Bible," Eric says. I asked why the girl/boy separation. He claimed the boys have too much energy. He separates the groups and uses the Reverend Walt Markham's Go for It material—heavily game- and activity-oriented—with these twelve- to thirteen-year-old boys.

Walk into the kindergarten through fifth grade boys and girls Sunday school at University United Methodist Church in Wichita. See the kids bubbling with enthusiasm. "They love it," says Kara Kuehnel, Christian education director. They use the One B.I.G. Room materials for this age spread. Physically the children occupy two rooms— one with a puppet stage and one with a TV equipped for playing videos and DVDs.

Come early and watch the children go to their own carpet squares to sit and sing or to stand for the dancing. The teachers exclaim, "There is so much to draw from." LIVE B.I.G. gives them lots and lots of options.

Kara claims, "They needed something different. The flexibility and interactive nature of the B.I.G. experience builds a whole new biblical and faith experience for the children."

New Approaches

With Sunday under attack, and even the best strategies for Sunday school struggling, can't churches devise other methods to "offer them Christ"?

Lots of churches have day care centers—a good social service that helps both working parents keep their jobs and support the family. But it is hard to teach a two-year-old a lot about the Bible. Some churches see only the social service aspect and let outsiders run their day care without a thought for Christian education. As a pastor, I noticed that the parents who dropped their kids off for day care never joined the church. Also, some after-school safe havens and many tutoring programs take the same tack—help a child, help a family— but never deal with faith, scripture, or Jesus Christ.

Why am I upset? Not because some churches are being helpful, even kind, but because they have forgotten the words of our Lord: "Let the little children come to me" (Mark 10:14). It's not good enough to put the children inside the church walls for a few hours. The question is: How can we help the children and their families come to a saving faith in the Lord? Maybe part of my problem is that I personally never developed a good method of integrating the parents of day care children with our church people or church life. My preschool was stronger—often taught by people of faith, often involving the parents more, often teaching four-, five-, and six-year-olds some scripture, some hymns, some prayers. I found that some of these families were already a part of the church. Other families joined our fellowship.

But, dear friends, we live in a secular society. For forty years, from 9 a.m. to 3 p.m., we've taught our children math and grammar, but not Moses and the prophets, not the Sermon on the Mount or the Lord's Prayer. For forty years we mainline Protestant churches accustomed to cultural reinforcement have been sitting on our hands, waiting for another train to come by. Truth is, if we want to reach the children with the love of Jesus, we must do it ourselves. Our Sunday schools are tired, old-fashioned, and in decline. We have to find a modern, enthusiastic way.

In our little town of Winfield, Kansas, I watch the Lutherans and the Roman Catholics do it with parochial schools. The Muslim and Jewish communities here are too small but, in nearby Wichita, they also have their own parochial schools.

Some of my conservative, evangelical friends have begun private, Christian schools. They argue they want their children to have a better education than the public schools can give—and they desire prayer and Bible instruction for their children.

My cynical mind notes that they remove their children from the poverty areas of the city and from most of the non-Anglo children, developing an unspoken form of segregation. But I bite my lip in silence.

They also vote for school vouchers, against taxes to strengthen public schools. Amazing to me, in Kansas, where we once fought the saloon, some of these private school parents even vote for gambling, claiming that some of the money will help public schools.

The saddest part of the story is that we mainliners stand by, wringing our hands, while poor children, black and Hispanic children, neighborhood children, and, yes, our children, grow up in a religious vacuum—in schools as secular as the Sahara Desert is dry. No wonder pastors trying to reach young adults print the Lord's Prayer in their Sunday bulletins. Where in school would they have learned it? Like a bull in a Kansas pasture, I stand on the other side of the fence. Maybe it's because my father served on the school board. Maybe it's because my daughter-in-law gives up every other Monday night, without pay, as a member of our local school board. Maybe it's because my wife and I, our children, and our grandchildren all are products of the public schools. Deep in my heart, rooted and grounded in near-sacred tradition, is my belief that every child in America—of every race, creed, or color—deserves a first-class education, the finest and best possible.

But I have two problems. First, the public schools are short of money. Thanks to old people who say their children are grown, to parents whose kids are in private schools, to young people who don't care, state after state is underfunding their school systems. The federal government has lost the vision too: the federal deficit stands like a giant ogre opposing everything from AmeriCorps and Pell Grants for college students to aid to states for elementary and secondary education. The result? In many school districts across the country, music, art, drama, even physical education—all are being cut back.

My second problem is bigger. If our churches' own Sunday schools are in decline and if our public schools are devoid of faith learning, how will the children come to know? How will they learn about Jesus and come to love him? Where will they learn? Who will teach them?

Lots of churches, God bless them, have a Wednesday program—choirs, children's after-school activities, family night dinners, classes. Good, but extremely limited in terms of strong Christian teachings, Bible study for children, or careful instruction in the ways of our faith.

School after School

So, without undermining the public schools, without rewriting the U.S. Constitution, without launching United Methodist parochial schools, what can we do? I'm pleading for "school after school"! I'm asking for Wesley's strategy of reaching children to be applied to modern America. What are the children's needs? When are the children available? How could we mobilize our resources to teach them? Why not use the Bible?

The answers:

When? Monday through Friday, 3:30 until 5:30 p.m.

Why? Parents are at work. (Ninety percent of mothers in both two-parent and one-parent households have jobs outside the home.) It's the highest crime rate time in the day. Many elementary and junior high children have nothing to do, no place to go.

Where? The church buildings with fabulous educational facilities generally stand empty, looking as quiet and lonely as a fraternity house on Saturday evenings.

Who? A battery of available people. Consider: college students in training to become educators, retired people including retired teachers, mothers and fathers whose children are involved and who could work part-time. A retired lawyer friend of mine spends some time each week listening to a third grader read. Many college students would love to work with children in music and art. Old literature teachers never die.

How? Some schools will transport the children to the church. Many churches have buses and vans. Parents can pick up their children after work.

Money? Look at the all-day parochial schools: they charge a modest tuition, give scholarships to the poor, give through the church, raise money with benefits. If you think this effort is too much work, try running a Lutheran or Catholic school all day, all week. And while you're at it, recall the words of our Savior, "Whoever causes one of these little ones who believe in me to sin" (even by neglect), "it would be better for him to have a great millstone fastened round his neck and to be drowned in the depth of the sea" (Matt. 18:6 RSV).

St. Luke's United Methodist Church in Houston has served families with after-school care since the 1960s. In addition to preschool and day care for small children, the church provides activities, love, and instruction for children—kindergarten through fifth grade. The strength, from my perspective, is that they have spotted the 3:30 to 5:30 p.m. window of opportunity. They provide restful recreation, snacks, tutoring, and homework areas. But, open to all children, including Jews, Muslims, and children of other Christian denominations, they go easy on biblical instruction. I talked to my friend Dr. Jim Moore, just before his retirement, and to his director, Sheila Bartram. They admit their strength is their weakness—open to all, they give a witness by their love and care, but hesitate to be too explicit with biblical material and Christian beliefs. They do offer prayer and prepare for Thanksgiving and Christmas celebrations. And they encourage the children to attend their vacation Bible school, Sunday school, and worship. But they respect the various backgrounds and traditions with minimal biblical instruction.

To my regret, as I look back over my own pastorates, love and care for children is not enough today. Now, with the tragic vacuum in biblical and spiritual knowledge, I believe we must be explicit. I believe we must tackle the afternoon hours by forming parochial schools after school. I believe we must be as deliberately intense and specifically Christian as we once were—and still try to be—with the Sunday school.

At St. Luke's, the school after school has been so successful (and working parents so desperate) that a summer school has been added—three months of classes and care from 7 a.m. to 6 p.m. It's been so successful that Jane Williams, director of children and family ministries, was chosen Early Childhood Educator of the Year for 2004 in Texas. So successful that other churches ask for advice and counsel; so successful that a two-day training event for teachers of young children drew 2,000 participants.

Just as the Wesleyans found a space in the schedule of poor working children—Sundays—so a potential gap for us could be 3:30 to 5:30 p.m. Monday through Friday. Many schools will deliver the children to the churches; most parents (or grandparents or neighbors or friends) can pick them up before 6:00 p.m.

Of course, schools after school must be relaxed, fun, and flexible. Children with pent-up energy from being in a schoolroom all day need opportunities to let off steam. Our schools after school can be relaxed, can fill in the gaps of art, drama, and music vacated by the public schools. We can be more like a vacation church school experience.

What an opportunity to sing "Jesus Loves Me," what a fun time to draw, color, and paste pictures of Jesus healing the paralyzed man (then visiting the local church-related hospital to show Jesus' healing influence). What a window of opportunity to play Bible games on the computer instead of shooting cops on video games. What a blessing to have some tutoring for struggling students—or a chance for others to do their homework.

Remember, the same free country that keeps us from foisting our faith on the general population provides the power that enables us, in our own churches, on a voluntary basis, to teach the bedrock, holy rudiments of our religion—no holds barred.

Recently I ate breakfast in a motel on Sunday morning, ready to preach in a distant city. The waitress, divorced, had two children at home. She waited tables every Sunday morning. Then I visited with the clerk at the desk. He had a child at home. The family-aged security officers spoke to me as I left. I drove by the mall's parking lot full of cars and thought of the salespersons. Then I drove past the filling stations, the convenience stores, and, finally by a factory that never closed.

In a tough secular world, if we are driven by an evangelical fervor, if we want children to learn the ways of Jesus, we must be wildly creative, fanatically innovative, and willing to labor like "a worker who has no need to be ashamed" (2 Tim. 2:15).

Jesus took little children in his arms and blessed them. We must do the same.

Chapter 8 / WORSHIP

O come, let us worship and bow down,

let us kneel before the LORD, our Maker!

(Ps. 95:6)

When I was a preacher, worship, for me, meant preparing and preaching the Sunday sermon. The organist could handle the prelude and postlude. In the country church, I picked the three hymns, gave the choir director sermon themes ahead of time, used the Apostles Creed and the Gloria Patri, and offered an extemporaneous prayer. Later, in a city church, I consulted with the choir director about the hymns, and had a lay person or associate pastor read the Scriptures. I was thrilled when the children's choir or youth choir sang songs of their own choosing. I hate the lectionary—too rigid, often irrelevant to the moment. I still think it drains the preacher's passion, like a leak in a bucket. But, with the church year to guide me, with sermon themes lined out for some months ahead, with specific dates for Holy Communion and baptism, my plan was clear and simple.

My task was to work hard building the sermons. I was like a cabinet-maker constructing a new desk or table every week. Sunday, inexorably, loomed before me as inevitable as the morning sunrise. My job was to be ready to preach. I studied top preachers and learned that I needed to hole up like a bear in a cave and prepare, so I set aside Thursdays to read, plan, write, and practice in order to be ready for Sunday. I wanted to be relevant and biblical.

When we added live worship on a major commercial television station, the pressure intensified—especially the need to be precise with the time. But this pressure was offset by the knowledge that, on a winter's day with snow drifting across the roads in western Kansas, old folks in wheelchairs, Catholics who went to Saturday or early Sunday mass, Baptist farmers who couldn't get out to church—thousands of them would be worshipping with us. But worship, for me, was still the same as the country church: select three hymns and prepare and preach the best I could.

When did things change? Like an ocean tide imperceptibly going from ebb to flow, meaningful worship in America modified, moved. As with a change in the weather, conditions are different today. Suddenly, my well-trained, highly-motivated, hardworking way of doing worship was as out of date as last year's bird's nest.

The New Look

My son-in-law, the Reverend Rob Fuquay, pastor for over a decade at Long's Chapel United Methodist Church at Lake Junaluska, North Carolina, emerges from a younger generation. I asked him to describe what it is like to prepare for and conduct worship today in a church trying to reach new people, especially young adults. Here's what he wrote:

"Who would have thought twenty years ago that we were on the verge of a worship revolution? There were perhaps hints of it from some of the emerging mega-churches in America and the afterglow of the charismatic movement of the seventies. But on the whole, this style of worship just described in the introduction seemed well suited to serve The United Methodist Church for generations to come.

"Then church consultants like Leonard Sweet and Bill Easum came on the scene, telling us that, in the coming generation, music would replace liturgy. People would worship from their hearts more than their heads. Folks would come to church looking for an experience. It was hard to understand what that meant. Then we began to see it. Mainline churches, serious about reaching the ever-growing population of unchurched folks, introduced contemporary worship with lots of praise music. Guitars and electric keyboards replaced the organ. Drum sets started appearing behind the handbell tables. Video projector screens accompanied the stained glass.

"Soon we added adjectives to our worship services like *traditional, contemporary,* and *blended.* There was confusion about the meaning of it all and why churches were making changes in music, liturgy, and style. Many have attacked the changes out of fear that what has been meaningful to them would be taken away. Perhaps in some places this has been true, especially where churches seeking to be relevant felt they had to abandon the old. Others said new worship forms were 'dumbing down' the church. And, again, in some places this was true, especially where churches were simply using gimmicks to attract the unchurched.

"But overall, the revolution in worship has brought new life to the church. It has allowed congregations to relate to people who might not have been reached otherwise. So what characterizes the changing trends of worship in churches that are yet still alive?

Relevant, Emotive Music

"First, great music is indispensable. Music has long been, and still is, a powerful medium for experiencing the gospel. Many great contemporary worship services find ways to present timeless, spiritual truths in ever-changing, relevant ways. Instead of singing a multitude of verses using passé words and staring into a book, many churches have discovered great energy using songs with fresh language, where people sing with uplifted head reading the words on a screen. Rather than using instruments seldom heard outside of church, congregations have found power in using instruments people hear on the radio every day like acoustic and electric guitars, keyboards, drums, saxophones, flutes, violins. In place of a 'hymn sandwich' service where songs are spliced between other acts of worship, many churches put more music in one place, allowing the words and melodies to create an experience that prepares the heart for prayer and for hearing and responding to God's word.

"This does not merely mean old hymns are replaced with new praise choruses. Some churches have found the familiar hymns to be incredibly meaningful in contemporary worship services. Adam Hamilton, senior pastor of the United Methodist Church of the Resurrection in Kansas City, says many of the unchurched coming in their doors stand a better chance of recognizing 'Amazing Grace' than they do 'Amazing Love.' But when they hear the old hymns sung in a relevant style they make two connections—familiarity with the words and familiarity with the instruments and melody. A drum beat and various instruments backing an old hymn can create a whole new experience of worship. Music sung in a relevant way communicates to someone that 'this church understands me.'

"Many faster-beat hymns and praise songs will involve clapping to the rhythm. It simply engages people at another level and adds to the feeling of experiencing worship and not just going through a ritual. Churches that have broken through taboos, like not clapping during a service, and are now allowing spontaneity in participation, have created an atmosphere of genuineness and aliveness. Whereas some people experience a 'holy presence' in stillness and silence, many today encounter that same 'holy presence' in the energy and authenticity of contemporary music.

"Bono, lead singer of U2, in a song called 'Vertigo' from their latest album, sings about the circumstances of this 'vertigo': 'It's everything I wish I didn't know. Except you give me something I can feel.' That is the cry of a generation today.

Interactive, Participatory Worship

"People want an experience. They hunger for transformation more than information. Churches that understand this well create worship services that invite participation. A key to this is *space*. For many years sanctuaries were created with high altars and pulpits and long, narrow naves. There would be great distances between preacher and people. Now sanctuaries are created more and more with a communal feel. Preachers aren't high or removed. They are closer to the people and often on the same level with them. There are no large pulpits to stand behind. The preacher might use a small podium to hold sermon notes. People can see each other. The communal space says we are not all together having individual experiences, we are all together sharing in a common experience.

"The need for community is great in our society. When VCRs became popular, some experts predicted it would be the end of movie theaters. Yet, today, millions still go to the movies. People still want to share experiences together. It is not just about being in a crowd. People can be in crowds and still be lonely. They want experiences that are shared and can enhance relationships.

"Churches that start an alternative worship service might move out of the sanctuary into the fellowship hall, because the space can be designed to create greater interaction. Services that get people talking with each other develop a sense of community. This is done during greeting times, but there are also other opportunities. Sometimes preachers tell the people during a message to turn to the person next to them and ask or say something. Following a benediction, people might be asked to speak to three or four folks as they leave, repeating some phrase from the theme of the day.

"One Sunday, I thought the service was rather sleepy, so I asked the people to tug on the ears of the ones sitting in front of them to wake each other up as preparation for hearing the scripture lesson. (It was actually an illustration of Isaiah 50:4, 'Morning by morning he wakens—wakens my ear...') One man tugged on the ears of a woman he had never met. They got to know each other and fifteen months later got married. He says, 'After I told the congregation that story I noticed our single people never miss a Sunday!'

Multi-Sensory Communication

"Preaching is paramount in churches with thriving congregations. In fact, many churches with great contemporary worship give more time for the sermon than in traditional services. What might be different is the style. The preacher's conviction and passion is imperative! Along with the importance of what a preacher says is the way he or she says it. This does not mean preachers have to be charismatic or perform colorful antics. It simply means people want to know whether preachers believe what they are saying. The freedom to communicate, looking at the people more than at a manuscript, helps to do this. Personal illustrations add weight to the reality of the message. But too much personal material takes the focus off of Christ. Too little leaves the message in the third person. The key is vulnerable, biblical, personal passion.

"Fewer people today are auditory learners. Television commercials bombard us with dozens of images in a few seconds. PowerPoint has changed the way presentations are made. Wise preachers take advantage of the media available today for communicating the gospel. This includes multimedia. Being able to show an illustration rather than tell it helps. For instance, a sermon on racism might include a clip from the movie *Remember the Titans,* where the white football player is visited in the hospital by his black teammate and they talk about how they moved beyond their prejudices. Or a sermon on family might use a clip from the recent remake of *Cheaper by the Dozen,* where the father makes a decision in his family's best interest rather than accepting a promotion. In fact, numerous resources, many on the Internet, reference movies for sermon illustration purposes.

"Churches with video projection capabilities assist a preacher in making sermons more experiential. While hearing a description of ancient Corinth, the congregation can view pictures of the city. A well-worn illustration about the fresh waters of Galilee and the static water of the Dead Sea can have new meaning as people see illustrations of what the preacher describes. Also, video projection is valuable for its symbolic value. A key image that fits the theme of the service can be on the background the entire service, reinforcing the message of the day. Even in traditional services this device is helpful. In many churches the key visual symbols are stained glass windows that never change. For the same money (and usually much less!) a congregation can purchase a great video projection system that allows them to have fresh stained glass and other traditional images each week.

"Another component of this style of communicating is the use of personal testimonies from the congregation as sermon illustrations. Rather than telling about a spiritual experience that happened in the life of somebody no one knows, invite a person from the congregation to come forward and tell her or his story. As Rick Warren says, people are more likely to buy what you are selling when they hear the testimony of a satisfied customer rather than the sales pitch of a professional marketer!

"In churches that use testimonies like this, the pastor may come to a key point in the sermon and then invite someone to share his or her experience. Usually the pastor or another person involved with worship has sat down with that individual ahead of time to go over the details of the testimony. This helps with clarity, helps make sure the spiritual power isn't lost in wordiness or lack of focus. It also assures there is no violation of integrity or confidentiality. To the person in the pew, a powerful testimony from a fellow Christian says Christ is real and active in this community.

"Involving the congregation in the message is also spiritually powerful. Some preachers put outlines of their messages in the bulletin with blanks so people can jot down notes and follow along. The people may be invited to read together key phrases or scripture verses being referenced in a sermon. For many it will be the only time they read the Bible that week! Some preachers pause after key points to say, 'Get it?' And the congregation responds, 'Got it!' And the preacher concludes, 'Good,' before continuing. It just helps keep people tuned in and involved in the sermon.

"Other multisensory aids might include props to illustrate points in a message. John Ortberg, former teaching pastor at the Willow Creek Community Church near Chicago, once illustrated the way God's word acts as a filter for our spiritual lives by showing the congregation the air filter from his furnace at home. His furnace had not been working and a repairman told him the problem: he had not been changing the filters. So Ortberg told the congregation what a clean filter should look like and showed them the dusty, black one taken from his house. Everyone moaned. Then he moved quickly into the way our souls can appear when we don't have regular filtering. He used a visual aid.

"One Father's Day, Mike Slaughter, senior pastor of Ginghamsburg United Methodist Church in Tipp City, Ohio, used the powerful sense of smell to draw people into thinking about their dads. He had the bulletins lightly sprayed with Old Spice. The point in effective preaching today is to make use of sensory mediums that connect God's word to people's lives. Allowing people to experience the truth of God's word can make the difference between their being 'doers of the word, and not merely hearers' (James 1:22).

Thematic Unity

"Thematic unity helps keep a worshipper connected throughout a service. Worship built around a common scriptural theme involves much time in planning. From the call to worship to the music to the message and the sending forth, everything harkens back to the theme. Ginghamsburg United Methodist Church began a service talking about Jesus as the 'capstone' with a video showing a group seeking to understand the meaning of a capstone. By the end of the video, everyone understood what a capstone was and a leader said to the congregation, 'Let's gather to worship today as we investigate how Jesus is a capstone who can hold life together.'

"Songs, symbols, children's messages, and prayers all connect and keep people focused. This is a different style of worship planning. It involves more than sitting in the study writing a sermon while the choir director picks anthems and hymns. It requires teamwork. It takes time. Advanced planning becomes essential. Adam Hamilton works two years ahead to give his worship planning group material to be thinking about. Some churches design bulletin covers to fit a certain series. Others create banners that go along with themes and seasons. Churches with gifted musicians write songs to match services. But like a central thread woven through a tapestry, there is thematic unity.

Creative Arts

"Finally, churches creating meaningful worship services learn to use well a variety of creative arts. Along with musical instruments and visual artistry, there are expressions like interpretive dance. Gifted dancers can design movements that help people experience the message of a scriptural passage. Willow Creek has a dance that follows the story of the persistent widow and the unjust judge. It leaves a congregation in tears.

"Another powerful art form is drama. Short, real-life vignettes that fit the theme of the day not only prepare people for a theme but make them want to hear the preacher speak! For instance, a message on confession of sin might start with a husband coming home from work one day and being confronted by his wife about her discovery of pornography sites that have been visited on their computer. Talk about creating a hush in a congregation!

"Dramas can also create outstanding humor because of the way they connect with people. A family life message can begin with a drama modeled after an old Carol Burnett Show skit with Ed and Eunice. Drama can also be a creative way to illustrate scripture. After reading the story of Abraham offering Isaac, one church had an older gentleman and a young teenager enact the story while a vocalist sang a moving song. The man literally lifted a butcher knife over the boy and then had his hand stayed as if by an angel. When he untied the boy's hands, there were tears not only in his eyes but in the eyes of every member of the congregation!

Excellence Is the Key

"The key to it all is doing worship with excellence. Many people who complain about not liking new and innovative worship services usually say so because what they experienced was not done well. A creative idea presented poorly is better not used. A drama where the people can't hear a speaker is useless. Contemporary music where the drums are louder than the vocalists is self-defeating. Use of movie clips not carefully cued or previewed can be disastrous.

"From good sound and lighting to appropriate flow—all are essential for meaningful worship. When done well, people respond much like they did in the Gospel of Mark: 'This amazed everyone and they praised God, saying, "We have never seen anything like this!" ' (2:12 NIV)."

After Rob's careful analysis, I asked our son, Paul, also a preacher struggling for authentic, relevant worship, to comment. He says:

"Dad, excellence in music, picture presentation, unity of theme— all are important, but they're not the whole story. I have had people get up and walk out of worship because drums were used—not poorly used, just used at all. I have had people complain bitterly because some folks clapped after a great anthem or stirring solo. They said the clapping noise was inappropriate in worship. It took their focus away from God.

"On the other hand, when the choir has worked hard to prepare a traditional cantata and give a powerful, excellent presentation, we lose some unchurched and some young worshippers who don't connect. The pastor gets criticized from both sides.

"One solution, of course, is the hamburger stand 'have it your way' approach. Some churches have traditional, conventional, contemporary, or formal services at different times or different places. Some pastors blend, often gently, with or without congregational consultation. Excellence is important. Communication is critical. Some conflict is inevitable.

"But the key is spiritual, theological. Does the congregation want to reach diverse, unchurched, new, and younger people for the Lord? Have the people lost sight of the command to make new disciples for Jesus Christ? Do they remember our Lord's teaching that we cannot put new wine in old wineskins (Matt. 9:17)?

"Embracing the new does not mean the old was bad but that changing times and the work of the Holy Spirit cannot be contained by older forms. When I served a previous appointment, the people gave me great latitude in worship because they were thrilled to see young people and children in the sanctuary again. We did not have the resources for different styles of worship, but as long as we were making new disciples, older folks who preferred traditional hymns and prayers were supportive.

"Now, in a larger congregation, we can successfully resource different forms of worship. (Note: In polling our last two membership classes, all but one of the twenty new members attended the contemporary celebration. Our eighth-grade confirmation class prefers it. Now our youth leadership team is rescheduling youth Sunday school [we call it church school] to the 11 a.m. hour so the youth can attend the 9:30 a.m. service that speaks to them.)

"Do you see the problem? Creative worship falls right into the 'have it your way' mentality of today's suburbia. And the 9:30 a.m. contemporary worship blows a huge hole in our Sunday school.

"Now we are developing an 11 a.m. church school for all ages (in addition to our 'traditional' 9:30 a.m. Sunday school). But the conflict crisis is significant. The congregation must decide—even while striving for excellent, meaningful, Spirit-filled worship—whether to reach for new disciples or protect the traditions of our long-term members. Doing both at the same time requires the skill of a Broadway tap dancer."

Reflecting on Rob's and Paul's comments, I'm almost glad I'm not a pastor anymore. I could handle all the worship changes personally, but I'm not sure I could deal with the criticism, the "I like this or that" confusion. I enjoy all music, from opera to country, from classic hymns to praise songs. I enjoy an enthusiastic songfest and I also love my sister's Episcopal high worship service with beautiful liturgy and glorious music.

The psalmist seems to understand our predicament:

> Praise ye the LORD.
> Praise God in his sanctuary: praise him in the firmament of his power.
> Praise him for his mighty acts: praise him according to his excellent greatness.
> Praise him with the sound of the trumpet: praise him with the psaltery and harp.
> Praise him with the timbrel and dance: praise him with stringed instruments and organs.
> Praise him upon the loud cymbals: praise him upon the high sounding cymbals.
> Let every thing that hath breath praise the LORD. Praise ye the LORD.
> (Ps. 150 KJV)

Chapter 9 / CONFLICT IN THE CHURCH

This is my commandment,
that you love one another as I have loved you.

(John 15:12)

In music, dissonance. In the springtime, stormy weather. In family life, arguments. In the church of Jesus Christ, differences of opinion, varied viewpoints, cataclysmic conflict.

Even under the ministry of Jesus, the disciples disputed. The apostles tried to send the noisy kids away. Jesus, like a wise parent, overruled them, saying, "Let the little children come to me" (Matt. 19:14). Peter didn't want his feet washed. Jesus insisted: "Unless I wash you, you have no share with me" (John 13:8). Judas condemned Mary for lavishly pouring out precious perfume on Jesus, wasting money that could have been given to the poor. Jesus rebuked him (John 12:5-8).

As the church was aborning, conflict erupted like a thunderstorm on a March evening. At first, they "were all of one mind." But, as some of the husbands were martyred, the number of widows increased. Some of the widows didn't get a fair shake in the daily food distribution. The old-timers—the Aramaic-speaking, Judean Jewish Christian women—got full portions. The outlanders—the Greek-speaking, Jewish Christian women—got shortchanged. After a church conference, Peter sent Stephen, Philip, and five others—all Greek-speaking Jewish Christians—to bring justice to bear (Acts 6:1-6).

Barnabas and Paul, the greatest of friends and coworkers, disagreed angrily over whether to take John Mark, Barnabas's nephew (or cousin) on the second missionary journey. John Mark got homesick and had abandoned them when the going got rough on the first trip. Barnabas believed the young man to be stronger, more grown-up now. Paul had no time for a wimp, a deserter. "The disagreement became so sharp that they parted company" (Acts 15:39). (One of the greatest biblical examples of reconciliation occurs years later when John Mark, now tough and steadfast, is with Paul who is in prison [Philemon 1:23].

The first really big church-wide explosion occurred when missionaries began converting non-Jews in Asia Minor (Acts 15). The Gentile men were uncircumcised. They and their families ate pork and shrimp, and carried wood and water on Saturdays. But they gave their hearts to Jesus as Lord and Savior and received the Holy Spirit. So the leaders called a church conference in Jerusalem. All the leaders came (Acts 15). Liberals and conservatives sat together, argued, and prayed. The hard right insisted, "Unless you are circumcised according to the custom of Moses, you cannot be saved" (Acts 15:1).

Impetuous Peter stood up and gave testimony. He recalled how he stayed in Joppa with Simon the tanner (think odor from the animal skins drying in the sun; think becoming "ceremonially unclean" according to Mosaic law). Peter told about his dream from God that took him to Cornelius, the Roman centurion. Peter related the conversion experience as the Holy Spirit was poured out on Cornelius and the entire Gentile gathering. Peter must have quoted his own words, "God shows no partiality" and again, "Can anyone withhold the water for baptizing these people who have received the Holy Spirit just as we have?" (Acts 10:34, 47).

Paul and Barnabas, the left wing, told of the fabulous conversions in Antioch where they started calling each other "Christians." They spoke of "signs and wonders" (Acts 15:12).

James, brother of Jesus, was a conservative. Tradition says he believed with all his heart that Jesus was the Savior sent from God the Father, but he went to the temple every day to pray and kept all the Jewish religious rituals and rules. (Tradition also says James was martyred by Jewish officials either by stoning or by being thrown from the temple tower before A.D. 70) After Paul and Barnabas explained, in glowing terms, the dramatic conversion of non-Jews in Antioch, James agreed to their inclusion. First, he quoted the prophets. But then he laid down some deep guidelines for compromise. New Gentile converts must abandon all forms of worshipping false gods. They must not drink blood, for blood contained life. (In Tarsus, initiates to Mithraic worship watched as a bull would be ritually slain. The new converts would stand under the platform, rub the blood in their eyes, their ears, their nostrils. Then they would drink the blood from a chalice, gaining life, strength, and invincibility from the bull's blood.)

New Gentile converts must also abstain from fornication and adultery—sexual sins scorned throughout the Torah. Years later, Paul said that James and the other leaders asked him to remember the poor in Jerusalem. Keeping that promise, and taking the offerings personally to Jerusalem, cost Paul imprisonment and death (Gal. 2:10).

After this huge debate in Jerusalem, unity was restored and the mission to make disciples exploded in all directions.

So often the church forgets the great prayer of Jesus. He prayed to the Father that "they may be one as we are one" (John 17:22 NIV). People who brag on the Bible should remember that. And, amid the confusion and conflict within the Corinthian church, we are to remember the majestic plea of St. Paul that "if I speak in the tongues of mortals and of angels, but do not have love, I am a noisy gong or a clanging cymbal" (1 Cor. 13:1).

Dr. Paul Tillich used to say that the greatest sin within Christendom is denominationalism. Like a stream hitting a rocky island, we often divide and go our own way whenever we disagree. John Wesley never wanted to leave the Church of England—never did—but the Methodist movement separated from the Church of England and the colonial Methodists also broke away. William Booth refused his Methodist appointment so that he could go to the ragtag and bobtail of London, later forming the Salvation Army. Again and again, with Wesleyan Methodists, Nazarenes, and Assemblies of God, splits occurred. Among Methodists, the 1844 division over slavery separated the South from the North and required over a century (1968) to heal.

Homosexuality

Some of my dearest friends want to split whole denominations over the issue of homosexuality. They say, separate, and let each viewpoint go its own way. I don't agree with them, even though I hold strong views on the matter of gay and lesbian believers in the church. Sometimes it takes half a century to work a matter through. Times change, attitudes modify, we see biblical passages in a new light. I remember when my grandmother quit wearing white gloves to church and when my wife quit wearing a hat. Now my granddaughter wears blue jeans to worship; some boys wear baseball caps in chapel. So let's keep talking, keep praying, keep loving: "as the Father has loved me, so I have loved you; abide in my love" (John 15:9).

We didn't have homosexuals in the old days. Recounting those days sounds like stereotyping. When I was growing up, people would ask Mrs. Smith, "Mary, where is that talented artist son of yours?"

"Oh, he's in New York, studying and trying to make a living painting portraits."

"Is he married?"

"No, no, he and another fellow are saving money, sharing a studio apartment."

Or, "Joann, is your daughter who used to sing in the choir still at home?"

"Oh, no, she moved to Los Angeles. She and another girl are trying to make the big time, singing in stage shows and movie choruses. They're singing in the church, too."

My grandmother was widowed at age fifty-two. She took in women schoolteachers to help pay the bills. The ladies lived in bedroom apartments upstairs. I guess she had women who lived together for thirty years. (In El Dorado, Kansas, school board rules forbade a single teacher to marry—they lost their job if they did.)

Later, I recall two women in Wichita who moved in together right after World War II—both young businesswomen. They became leaders in the Wesleyan Service Guild (the Professional Church Women). They were our communion stewards. You would find them in the church kitchen washing communion cups long after midnight on Christmas Eve. When they were in their nineties, one became an invalid; the other gave her sips of water and put chips of ice in her mouth until she died. They were committed to the Lord, to the church, and to each other.

Out on the farms, we often had families with four or five children. As they grew up, the sons and daughters married. But occasionally, one son would stay at home with the folks. He never dated, never married. You'd see him drinking coffee with the fellows at the village café or sitting alone in church. He never seemed interested in women. Sometimes, he'd be gone for a couple of weeks on vacation.

It used to be, when two women sang in the choir together, or when the organist ate lunch with the lead tenor, we didn't think a thing about it. We knew them, called them by name, loved them. When people are friends and neighbors, prayer partners in a Bible study group or church school class, we don't label them Hispanic or Asian or Black or gay. They are George or Sally, Pete or MaryBelle—not categories.

I was slow as a Missouri mule in even thinking about homosexuals. Oh, I knew that in two of my churches there were a couple of young men who were top scholars, musicians, good-looking men, presidents of the youth fellowships. Everybody liked them. But they didn't date. Both died of AIDS, one after going to Yale and singing with the Whiffenpoofs.

I was so slow that at General Conference of 1984 I voted for the phrase "in marriage, fidelity, in singleness, celibacy." Like many folks, I saw single bars portrayed on television, heard of promiscuous sex by gay and lesbian people, began to read about the emerging controversy. But the entire matter seemed to be off in California or New York or somewhere else. As bishop of Arkansas, I had a few adultery problems by heterosexuals to deal with, but never an issue with homosexuals.

When did men and women begin to come out of the closet? And why? My wife, Julia, soft-spoken on these issues, mentioned that she had a male cousin, a pharmacist, who never married and had a special male friend all his adult life.

I will never forget being subpoenaed by the church court in Seattle, Washington. The appointed judge said I would be kicked out of the church if I didn't show. One of the jurors asked me what the Bible said about marriage. I don't think I was being flippant when I remembered a variety of biblical experiences: Father Abraham had one wife and one concubine; Jacob, father of Israel's twelve tribes, had two wives and two concubines; King David had numerous wives and concubines; Solomon had seven hundred wives and three hundred concubines. St. Paul urged men not to marry at all but give their lives to the gospel. Peter married. Jesus said some men are born eunuchs; others choose to be. And Jesus warned zealously against adultery (Matt. 5:27-28).

As for coming out of the closet, I was asked to speak at the Hearts on Fire Conference sponsored by the Reconciling Ministries Network and held at Lake Junaluska, North Carolina, in 2005. While I was standing in a hallway, perky, petite Reverend Beth Stroud came up to me. Her trial and appeal as a "self-avowed, practicing homosexual" was still alive in Pennsylvania. She grinned and said to me, "You are responsible for all my problems." I swallowed deep and asked for more data. Still smiling, she said she had been an effective pastor for several years; she had a partner; the church loved and supported her. But then she began to take DISCIPLE Bible study. And every week, every day, she felt challenged to have total integrity, to not be a hypocrite, to be open and aboveboard with God and everyone. So, she acknowledged to the church, the bishop, and the world that she and another woman were faithful partners. Then the sparks began to fly, and she lost her ordination. Well, I hugged her and cried a little, and blamed the Holy Spirit.

The Bible

For the past twenty years, I've been especially eager to understand the Bible. I'm so troubled by those who never read it, and by those who claim to read it, claim it to be inerrant, yet use it to fortify their prejudices. I want to spend the rest of my life helping inform the ignorant, and helping scriptural students read with the spirit of Jesus. I confess I am a "Jesus Christian" for "no one can say 'Jesus is Lord' except by the Holy Spirit" (1 Cor. 12:3 NKJV). I'm convinced certain portions of scripture—Mosaic laws regarding kosher food, Sabbath observance, and temple worship—helped crucify our Savior.

Two distinguished Bible scholars, Richard Hays of Duke University and John Holbert of Perkins School of Theology at Southern Methodist University, say authoritatively that no word meaning "homosexual" or "homosexuality" appears in the Bible, not in Hebrew or Greek.

Some point to the destruction of Sodom, in Genesis, because somewhere along the line the word "Sodomite" began to be used. But Sodom, in a society where hospitality was sacred, was guilty of violent, gross, unheard-of inhospitality. The angry, lustful townspeople were eager to rape, violate, maim, and kill the strangers—be they men or women—who were visiting Lot. "This was the guilt of your sister Sodom: she and her daughters had pride, excess of food, and prosperous ease, but did not aid the poor and needy" (Eze. 16:49). Jesus implied that Sodom was guilty of ugly inhospitality in Luke 10:10-12.

The Old Testament is in constant tension, trying to be both exclusive and inclusive. The holiness code in Leviticus and Deuteronomy tried to create a set-apart people—distinct from the Canaanites. But the prophets, and sometimes human experience, argued otherwise. For example, the holiness code denied access to the temple to someone maimed or castrated (Deut. 12:1), yet Isaiah demanded the opposite: castrated men and foreigners were welcome (Isa. 56:4-5). I've been fascinated by the fact that Philip the evangelist converted and baptized a black, foreign eunuch. The holiness code prohibited marriage to a pagan foreigner. Remember, Ezra made Jewish men divorce their non-Jewish wives. Moabites were forbidden in the temple "even to the tenth generation" (Deut. 23:3). Yet Ruth, the Moabite, became the wife of Boaz, leaning on the rules of *Levirate* marriage. She became the great-grandmother of King David.

Earlier I suggested that Jesus attracted crucifixion by challenging food laws, Sabbath rules, and temple veneration. Those Hebrew scriptural rules and their interpretations put our Lord on the cross. Jesus also offended religious authorities by his radically inclusive ministry. Jesus seemed to gravitate to the outcast, the left out, even to the hated. Luke, the non-Jew, alone recorded Jesus' answer to the lawyer's question, "Who is my neighbor?" Our Lord said the hated Samaritan picked up the injured man, dressed his wounds, and carried him to an inn. He was neighbor. (We can't even imagine how the Jews and Samaritans hated each other. Why, if a Samaritan left a footprint in the mud, a Jew would put dry straw in the footprint and set fire to it.)

The Samaritan woman at the well had been married five times. Perhaps she couldn't bear children and was dumped by every husband. The leper was a social outcast. Levi, a tax collector for the Roman occupation forces, was called into "the twelve." Zacchaeus, a chief tax collector, ate lunch with the Master, dumbfounding the crowd.

The toughest passage for Bible readers to swallow are the words of St. Paul in Romans 1:24-28. Paul said that men having sex with men, women with women, was "an abomination." What does he refer to? He's not writing about homosexuality as we know it. He's commenting on the fallen nature of humankind. "They became futile in their thinking, and their senseless minds were darkened" (Rom. 1:21). We creatures ignore the Creator and then passionately make ourselves the objects of our own veneration. We can fall into the sexual practices of our pagan world.

Corinth, a busy, overcrowded seaport city, was renowned for its sexual promiscuity. In fact, it was known as "sin city." The Athenian satirist Aristophanes used "to corinthianate" to euphemize "to fornicate." Plato spoke of "a Corinthian girl" when he meant a prostitute.

Paul saw, in the bars and back alleys of Corinth, heterosexuals passionately doing all manner of sexual aberrations. He also watched men and women parade to the pagan temples to have sex with the priests and thus ensure fertility for their farms. Workers on the land wanted their barley fields to flourish; herdsmen wanted their sheep to multiply. So they made their way to the fertility gods in various temples where male and female priests served as divine mediators. The sex acts, men with women, men with men, women with men, women with women, were performed by heterosexuals to ask favors of the gods.

The temple to Aphrodite in Corinth sat high up on the hill and housed over 1,000 sacred prostitutes. Paul watched the daily stream of worshippers ascend the hillside. Also, Paul knew of rich patriarchs in Athens who took young boys into their homes as playthings. The men—prominent heads of families and even philosophers—were pedophiles, like that occasional Roman Catholic priest who has tragically played around with altar boys. The men committed sins against children, the very children our Lord gathered into his loving arms.

Our problem is exacerbated by changing social conditions. Like sands shifting on the seashore, times and customs change. In Bible times, marriage was economic. The family inheritance depended on a male heir. Marriages were arranged; girls married soon after puberty, boys at age sixteen or seventeen when they could assume responsibilities. Survival needed the family farm. No time for a girl to think, "Do I like boys?" or for boys to ask, "Do I like girls?"

Today, in America, both women and men go to college, get jobs, move from city to city, often not marrying until they are thirty, thirty-five, or even forty years of age.

One woman, who took a partner when she was in her early thirties, told me she knew when she was fourteen that she was not interested in sex. She had dated some for show in college, for friendship as a working adult. Then she rented an apartment, tried living alone, and became lonely, depressed, near suicidal. She met a woman and fell in love. They had a pastor say a prayer over them in a pasture, and are committed partners to this day.

A young man walked out of worship with his partner and handed me his testimony. It read:

> When I was seven or eight years old, my Grandmother Godbey "knew" God was calling me into the ministry. She and God had coffee together every morning in the kitchen and she just "knew."
>
> Grandma gave me a copy of *Stories of Jesus,* where everything that Jesus said was written in red. I asked why. Grandma smiled and said Jesus' words are very important. The red is to make sure we'd pay attention.
>
> Then she and I sat down under the shade of an oak tree as she told me the rest of the story—how Jesus showed love and mercy when he went to the cross and died for me. The red represented the blood he shed on Calvary. She quoted John 3:16. With tears on her cheeks, she asked me, "Andrew, do you want to give your life to Jesus?" My life changed completely that day when I said yes! My journey of faith had begun.
>
> As the years flew past, I not only discovered a love of the scriptures, but also an incredible love of music. I found I could "preach" with music. There's something to be said about Southern Baptist folks. They know a gift when they see one, and they know how to encourage!
>
> In high school I sang in the church choir, occasionally performing a solo. Grandmother was in the congregation. Somewhere in there I realized I was gay.
>
> Then I spent a year at a wonderful theological school in southern Missouri called Evangel College. After intensive Bible study, I was convinced that God was calling me to a ministry overseas. So I joined the Navy to ensure that would never happen. But after two years in the Navy, I found myself heavily involved in a wonderful Assembly of God congregation in Naples, Italy.
>
> However, the fact I was hiding in the closet was never far from my thoughts. If being gay is a horrible sin, I found myself praying, begging my heavenly Father to change me, heal me, deliver me. Jesus said that if we asked for a piece of bread, would God give us a stone? Why was I crying myself to sleep, begging God to do something I knew I had absolutely no control over?

I'd been told (preached to) how "these people" chose this lifestyle. Believe me, I never chose to be gay. Why would I choose to ostracize myself from the one thing that gave me a purpose in life: my church? Why would I choose to live in fear of being kicked out of the Navy? Why would I choose to live in a community with the highest risk of HIV/AIDS? Why would anyone choose to live a life that could potentially get him or her kidnapped, tied to a fence post, and beaten to death?

I have come to the realization that, for whatever reason, I was created gay. Why? I don't know. When we all get to heaven and stroll down the golden avenue with Jesus, we'll ask him why. However, down here—right now—I'm going to keep telling my gay brothers and sisters who Jesus really is. The Jesus who didn't find the issue important enough to address. The Jesus who said, "For God so loved the world that he gave his only Son, that whoever believes in him should not perish, but have everlasting life" (John 3:16 RSV).

We Kansans are red-faced-embarrassed when we read about the Reverend Fred Phelps waving signs across the country that read, "God hates FAGs." It reminds us that Adolf Hitler marched homosexuals into the gas chambers even before he persecuted the Jews. Hatred, like poison in drinking water, is a deadly matter.

Scientists have been studying this issue for a long time. Dr. Evelyn Hooker, beginning in the 1950s, spent a quarter of a century testing homosexual men and proved they were as mentally healthy as heterosexuals. In 1973, the American Psychiatric Association removed homosexuality from its list of sociopathic disorders. In 1975, the American Psychological Association supported that decision, stating, "Homosexuality per se, implies no impairment in judgment, reliability, or general social and vocational capabilities" and we "must take the lead in removing the stigma of mental illness long associated with homosexual orientation." Scientists estimate that between 3 and 8 percent of the population is gay/lesbian.

On this whole issue of homosexuality, I have been helped tremendously by Peter Gomes in his *The Good Book*. Dr. Gomes is professor of Christian morals at Harvard. He's also black and gay. While affirming that homosexuality is a state of createdness, not a voluntary choice, he, nevertheless, like James at that early Christian conference, raises a red flag against sexual sins that are often thrown in the same box with faithful gay and lesbian unions. He has a lifetime partner, but he insists that does not fling open the door to "everything" as some people argue.

To affirm that gay men and lesbian women can love Christ Jesus and be filled with the Holy Spirit does not mean the church affirms lasciviousness, promiscuity, and exploitation—by anyone. To acknowledge that God-created persons who openly express their form of homosexuality in a "loving, monogamous, and faithful" relationship does not imply acceptance of pederasty or prostitution (p. 162).

I believe James, the brother of Jesus, would be proud of these distinctions. I believe Paul would again affirm persons who reveal the fruits of the Spirit: "love, joy, peace, patience, kindness, goodness, faithfulness, gentleness and self-control" (Gal 5:22-23 NIV).

Love and Unity in the Church

Many of my close associates in the church will see this issue and the scriptures differently than I do. That's life. Can you imagine how complicated this matter will be—for a long time into the future?

A pastor asked me whether he should baptize an adopted baby presented by two faithful women in his church. Another pastor baptized a baby born through artificial insemination to a loving mother and jointly loved by a two-mother union.

Should we conduct a funeral in the church for a young college student who died of AIDS? Should we allow a gay man who sings in our choir to join The United Methodist Church? Should some congregations become "reconciling congregations"—a haven for parents of gay children—and other congregations form a "confessing movement," declaring homosexuality a sinful act, not a state of being? Should we permit a pastor to perform a covenant union service for homosexuals or even a marriage in states where it is legal, or offer a prayer in states where it is not?

Should we allow a faithfully "yoked" pastor to maintain her or his ordination? Should a congregation hire a defrocked gay pastor to be a lay minister? Should we allow a lesbian United Church of Christ minister to serve a United Methodist congregation? Should United Methodists, like the Episcopalians, elect a gay bishop?

My wife, Julia, has just placed a bumper sticker on her car. It reads, "I believe in the separation of church and hate!" Like the disciples and church leaders gathered in Jerusalem, can we hold together in love?

I've noticed that, with a few exceptions, local congregations handle this issue (and many others) better than political church arenas like the General Conference. Why? Because when matters get close-up, face-to-face—faith and love take charge and categorizing and philosophizing diminish. Here's an example.

In Arkansas I went, as bishop, to a big anniversary celebration in a small, conservative village church—far off the beaten track. A young man came out from Little Rock to play the piano for the service. After church, everyone spoke to him, some laughed and hugged him, thanking him for coming. He had grown up in that church. Some of his Sunday school teachers remembered childhood antics. Julia visited with him, found out that his partner had stayed home in Little Rock. I visited with his mother, who was president of the United Methodist Women. The young man was gay, but nobody cared. He was flesh and blood, a real person, one of their own. He loved the church; he loved them; he loved Jesus Christ.

The closer our Lord Jesus came to the crucifixion, the more intensely he called for us, his followers, to care for one another. Like a mother on her deathbed who gathers all her children around her, giving them love and last-minute guidance, so Jesus, in his last days, told his disciples to love one another. On the dusty trails of Galilee, he had instructed disciples to feed the hungry and heal the sick. But with Calvary's cross on the horizon, our Lord focused on the center of the center. "Your love for one another will prove to the world that you are my disciples" (John 13:35 NLT). In the Upper Room, immediately after Jesus had washed the apostles' feet and given them wine and broken bread, he quietly said, "Just as I have loved you, you also should love one another" (John 13:34). In his Great Prayer, recorded in John's Gospel, our Lord prayed for us and for our unity: "I ask not only on behalf of these, but also on behalf of those who will believe in me through their word, that they may all be one" (John 17:20-21).

The Reverend John Danforth, former U.S. ambassador to the United Nations, addressed Episcopalian leaders in June 2006 at the General Convention of the Episcopal Church, meeting in Columbus, Ohio. Responding to the turmoil in the church over a gay bishop, Danforth stated, "A broken church is a sad church. . . . I believe that at the parish level, there should be all kinds of forums and sermons and material available on the subject, and I think that our great thinkers should help us reclaim the ministry of reconciliation."

In this book I'm pleading for us to make disciples. Let us give heed to our beloved teacher's deepest prayer: "As you, Father, are in me and I am in you, may they also be in us, so that the world may believe" (John 17:21).

I only remember one controversial sermon preached when I was a seminary student. Dr. Browne Barr, a relatively young new professor who had recently suffered the death of his wife, stood up in Battel Chapel at Yale Divinity School and preached on Galatians 6:10 (RSV): "Do good to all men, and especially to those who are of the household of faith." He stressed love within the church prior to love to the world. In the coffee hour that followed, some idealistic students were angry, expressing bitter rebuttals, claiming that we should love everybody! Everybody the same—all the time, everywhere. I listened, but across the years, I have discovered that St. Paul and Dr. Barr are right: if there is love within the fellowship, then we can love those in the world. If there is discord and dissension among the disciples in the church, we have absolutely nothing to offer to a lonely, disillusioned, and sin-sick society.

We need today to reaffirm John Wesley's sermon "Catholic Spirit":

Though we cannot think alike, may we not love alike? May we not be of one heart, though we are not of one opinion? Without all doubt, we may.... Every wise man, therefore, will allow others the same liberty of thinking which he desires they should allow him; and will no more insist on their embracing his opinions, than he would have them insist on his embracing theirs. He bears with those who differ from him, and only asks him with whom he desire to unite in love that single question, "Is thy heart right, as my heart is with thy heart?"

John's brother Charles put it to music:

Celestial charity expands
The heart to all our ransom'd race;
Though knit to one in closest bands,
Her soul doth every soul embrace.
She no unkind exception makes,
A childlike follower of her God;

The world into her *heart* she takes,
The purchase dear of Jesu's blood.

Fanny Crosby, blinded as a child by poor medicine, wrote a hymn in the Salvation Army hymnbook called "There Is Room at the Cross." It closes like this:

At the cross there is room,
The millions have come.
There is still room for one.
There's room at the cross.

Today I think she would say, gay or straight, room for you, room for me—at the cross there is room.

Chapter 10 / COMMUNICATION

All who believed were together and had all things in common....

They broke bread at home

and ate their food with glad and generous hearts.

(Acts 2:44-46)

In the computer age, I'm a dinosaur. I don't even type well. When I mess up on my e-mail, I get my grandson Joel to come straighten things out. He treats me with a respectful deference, like a polite mechanic who would repair my car.

I know how to turn on my TV with a remote so we can watch the evening news. Like everyone, I watched Katrina rip New Orleans apart like an angry pack of wolves tearing up a carcass. I know how many points the Dow Jones average declined today, how a violent explosion rocked an Iraq mosque. Within hours, I can discuss last night's football game between the Chiefs and the Cowboys. I can tell you how many golf tournaments Tiger has won.

We live in an age of communication. The college kids know it so much better than I do. At Southwestern College in Winfield, Kansas, all main-campus students receive a wireless laptop when they enroll, right along with their room key and meal ticket. I see students sitting on a wooden bench under an old maple tree, drawing up information from the Library of Congress. At night they play computer games with students from Singapore or Brazil. Or they buy on eBay, blog with a *New York Times* editor, or e-mail a friend down the street.

Last summer we took grandson Joel and a college friend to Alaska. The trip ended with a five-hour wait at the Anchorage airport. The boys wanted to play frisbee golf. So while I went to the bathroom, they cell phoned a friend in Winfield. He quickly looked up on his computer the frisbee golf course in Anchorage and got the telephone number and address of the course. They grabbed an airport taxi. When I returned they were on their way. The entire communication took about five minutes.

Have you read *The World Is Flat* by Thomas L. Friedman? He traveled to India to visit with the young women who answer your phone when you order a country music classic by Johnny Cash or Willie Nelson—a DVD advertised on TV. Young women in Honduras can explain what went wrong with your credit card bill. Friedman tells how accountants can send your tax information to India or Korea at 5:00 p.m. and have your complete 1040 form on their desk at 8:00 the next morning. Communication is instant—around the world.

The Church

In bold, stark-naked contrast, the average church member doesn't know what is going on in the church at large—unless some scandal or controversy has weaseled its way into the secular news. Church folks may have read how many millions of dollars the Catholic bishop in Boston had to pay in a pedophile case. Or they read about how a preacher in Virginia refused membership to a gay Presbyterian who sang in his choir. But the great and glorious work of the church at home and abroad is a vacuum in their experience.

I asked our son, Steve, who teaches an adult Sunday school class in our church, whether he knows any active missionaries. He looked at me strangely and said, "How would I know?" We always pay our apportionments and support the system, but the system does not build relationships. The General Board does not send missionaries to visit our church, shake our hands, tell us about the clinic where they do surgery or the school where they teach bright-eyed children.

As a retired bishop, I get the *United Methodist Reporter* and the official church magazines. I read the *Newscope* headlines on my e-mail—but that news is not reaching most of the pastors or the laity.

The theory is that information comes from the top down—like a pre-radio or pre-TV society. But those days are gone forever. As Friedman insists, it is now person-to-person, face-to-face, immediate.

From time to time, some high-powered church officials will meet with the bishops and share valuable information. Good. But no matter how hard bishops try, the information can't trickle down to the local pastor, let alone to the folks in the pew.

I called our conference office to see how many people in each church even receive the conference paper (which is mostly limited to conference news). Answer: the pastor and six to a dozen lay persons.

Arkansas, now united into one United Methodist conference, aggressively has moved into the digital age. If you give your e-mail address to headquarters in Little Rock, they will send you news of United Methodist Church doings throughout the state of Arkansas. Most United Methodist preachers and some lay leaders are on the list. So about 5 percent of Arkansas United Methodists receive church news, but it is mostly about Arkansas.

The top-down strategy has several basic flaws. Leaders are trying to get their message out but don't know how. They either use their own limited vehicles or appeal to national publications. Those publications, in turn, decide what to report.

Second, most information—such as new church starts in Zimbabwe, Christian churches burned down by Islamic radicals in Indonesia, United Methodist Committee on Relief (UMCOR) "hands-on" work in Mississippi, or seminary applicants turned on by *Disciple* Bible Study—goes, in volume, to bishops, much to district superintendents and conference directors, and some to pastors who care to dig it out of magazines and church newspapers, but little gets to the eight million church members.

Third, in a world of minute-by-minute information, most church news is weeks if not months after the fact. Almost everything is in newsprint, available only after the excitement has passed like last month's snowstorm.

The average Joe or Jane, faithfully worshipping each Sunday, knows which members of the congregation are in the hospital and they remember the date for the youth fund-raiser, but that's about all.

One exception is found in a few independent church leaders who take advantage of radio and television. James Dobson, Robert Schuller, and others, saw the power of using the communication tools of the culture. Will the mainline denominations let the Internet and all of its related communication tools be scooped up by others as well?

A Place for the Personal

In a moment we'll be dealing with computers: home pages, degree plans online, links with church institutions, courses for spiritual and professional growth. But remember also that church folks are starving for face-to-face encounters, like football fans lined up to shake hands with the quarterback. When Martin Buber wrote *I-Thou,* he distinguished between I-It and I-Thou. As human beings we relate to things (I-It), but we must also relate to one another and to the Lord (I-Thou). People have grown weary of paying apportionments but never meeting a missionary; supporting a college but not visiting with a student or professor; paying money, like taxes, but not knowing where the money goes. The laity in the church today are hungry to connect.

When they take the initiative, miracles happen. It's possible, once again, to have a missionary relate to your congregation. Remembering the old days of Advance Special yokes, churches can have "their own missionary." First United Methodist Church in Wichita, Kansas, recently entertained Drs. Lynn and Sharon Fogelman, formerly in Kenya, now at Red Bird Mission in Kentucky. The church celebrated a Mission Sunday. The congregation pays $2,500 a year toward the Fogelmans' support in a "covenant relation program." Dr. Lynn Fogelman is a native Kansan, not a name drawn out of a hat. Three hundred people had lunch with the Fogelmans when they visited the church.

The United Methodist Church in the state of Missouri teamed up with Mozambique for several years of support and friendship relationships. People even traveled back and forth. Under Bishop Crutchfield's leadership, Arkansas is relating face-to-face with the Congo. Many other areas are developing a travel friendship and specific support base with overseas conferences.

The bishops of North Carolina are asking each church to take *Disciple* training and strengthen small-group ministries. Some pastors are raising the bar for new members: if you want to join this congregation, you will need to be in a small group for study and fellowship. Imagine the intimacy of two dedicated laymen holding hands in prayer with a dozen prison inmates. We're relearning how to personalize, how to connect. But massive, church-wide communication demands more, much more.

Institutions

Somewhere in the mid-twentieth century, the church and church institutions of higher learning began to drift apart. Some church colleges set out to be independent private colleges acknowledging "historic denominational roots." Some United Methodist colleges aspired to be powerful academic schools like Connecticut Wesleyan or Grinnell or Oberlin—no longer "church related." Some faculty did not want religious ideas infiltrating their views of secular philosophy or scientific inquiry. Many of the faculty were frankly agnostic. School officials did not want church leaders messing with their strategic decisions. Required chapel went out the window during Vietnam, never to return. Above all, the colleges did not want to be a "religious school" like Oral Roberts or Liberty University.

The churches drifted too. Parents were more than proud that their students went to the state universities where exciting football games were played. As a pastor, I paid apportionments and sent the colleges names of my high school students, but I did not know much about what was happening on their campuses. My sons played basketball for Southwestern College. I attended their games, I was involved as a parent, but I don't remember being involved in pastor's workshops or ethical/religious discussions, or musical and theatrical events. We didn't take our youth groups to visit the campus.

Like children growing up and leaving home, then moving to far-off places, the churches and the church colleges became distant. Only a trickle of money and a tip of the hat at Annual Conference reminded folks of the relationship.

But in the 1980s and 1990s, the winds shifted—all across the country. Sensing the drift in Arkansas, the new president of Hendrix College, Dr. Ann Die, visited each United Methodist district in the state, saying "We're going to be a top-flight, academic, United Methodist college—what's the problem?" Dr. Die was reaching out to the connection. People sat up and took notice. They started sending more money to the college. Dr. Die requested two of our strongest pastors to head religious life on campus; at the same time, the college pushed academic excellence. A scholarship program aimed at United Methodist students was called "U.M. Leadership Scholarships," and it caught the fancy of the churches. Renewed religious activity, including mission trips and ecumenical outreach, caught the eye of the Lilly Foundation, and Hendrix received a huge grant. Lectureships, laity honors, serious discussions, and musical and dramatic events drew people from all denominations and from United Methodist churches across the state.

Pfeiffer College in North Carolina, realizing the desperate need for money for private colleges, spearheaded a church/church college relationship in the entire Southeastern Jurisdiction, working toward a $1,000 per church grant to the church college in their area. Lots of meetings; lots of church/college discussion; lots of "let's strengthen the tie that binds."

It began at Southwestern College about fifteen years ago. First, the careful selection of a few faculty and staff, beginning with a Christ-centered John Wesley Fellow, Steve Rankin. A new philosophy professor was supportive. Cheryl Rude developed a nationally recognized leadership program stressing Christian principles. Voluntary chapel, with contemporary music, mostly student-led, was Spirit-filled—with first 50, then 100, then 150 students, faculty, and staff in attendance.

Cheryl's husband, Martin, built small outreach teams like Selah, a praise and worship group; Keynotes, a ten-member vocal ensemble; Living (Psalm) 150, an instrumental ensemble; the World Witness Team, a group of international students; and other groups that all witness in churches. Scholarships are now offered to all active United Methodist students with a B average. DISCIPLE Bible study was offered aggressively, both with college credit and without. A DISCIPLE program nurturing students' calls to a wide range of ministries is now directed by Ashley Alley. Many church colleges have sent work teams to Greensburg, Kansas; New Orleans; and impoverished areas all over the world. The experience is two-way: students both help and learn.

Southwestern College was selected to offer college credit online to the U.S. Army in religious studies. Building on that experience, the college now offers online courses aimed at youth workers and Christian educators—master's degrees in leadership and in specialized ministries. Many of these students are hard at work with youth groups and Sunday schools and could never go to a seminary. Visit sckans.edu/campusgraduate or beadisciple.com for both academic and extracurricular information.

I was appointed by the church and the college as "bishop in residence," and I help where I can, including the recruitment of Bishop's

Scholars, top Christian students from other countries. Small but significant grants send students to training conferences. Graduates going on to seminary jumped from nearly none to three to six a year! (The bishops in residence programs for retired bishops in colleges and seminaries has become a valuable linkage: Bob Morgan teaching religious studies at Birmingham Southern, Bob Fannin raising money for Florida Southern, Don Wilson advising ministerial students at Southwestern University in Texas.)

A New Future

Churchwide, leaders are trying. The Disciples of Christ denomination is producing a new publication. Newscope, from the United Methodist Publishing House, sends out a weekly e-mail of headline issues. Some aggressive bishops put speeches and important announcements on conference web pages.

In a person-to-person, immediate communication age, the most aggressive stroke is a new strategy of the *United Methodist Reporter*. The publication, based in Dallas, is an independent, not-for-profit entity, originally designed to connect the local church news with conference and denominational news. The *Reporter* maintains a weekly connection with 120,000 homes across the country.

But the big news is their new portal home page designed for every household in a congregation. It can even include visitors and prospective members.

Imagine that you are Joe and Mary Smith, twenty-four years old, joining the church on Easter. You open your church's home page to get the Yahoo headlines and do Google searches. Faster than the six o'clock news, you see on the left side of the page the pastor's sermon for next Sunday with suggested scripture readings, and the fact that Mary Johnson has requested prayers for her breast cancer surgery this morning. You can give right then and there with a credit card. You read that the youth are planning a missionary work trip to Juarez, Mexico, during spring break—donations needed. You note that blood pressure testing will be available at the church on Thursday, 2-4 p.m.

You are a regular Joe or Jane in the congregation, but before you have shaved or put on your make-up you know just as much about the church family as your pastor does.

"How can this be?" you ask. The church secretary, even in the tiniest rural church, or any volunteer in his or her home, simply types it in as the news becomes available, and it immediately shows up on the home page for your congregation. It takes five minutes to type it in—to type in most of the material that might appear in next Sunday's bulletin. But remember, Sunday is days away—after Mary Johnson has gone home from the hospital, after the blood pressure clinic is over. Remember, too, that two-thirds of the membership will not be in worship reading the announcements next Sunday.

Big News

But the fast-breaking big news—the kind that would be on a church-owned CNN or CBS—is on that home page too. It works like this:

Front and center, you see a fast-breaking story. The drought in Oklahoma is spawning raging prairie fires, threatening homes, and burning churches. A malaria outbreak in Mozambique reaches epidemic proportions. North Korea boasts of nuclear capabilities, increasing international tension.

Then, immediately, to the side, stands the church response. Hundreds of volunteer firefighters from local farms and villages aid the professionals. Churches have opened their doors to burned-out families. Bishop Joao Somane Machado of Mozambique heads the Malaria Coalition of churches and international governments to combat that disease. The World Methodist Conference will meet in Seoul, Korea, in June. Leaders will travel to North Korea pleading for consultation on nuclear weaponry and praying for peace.

Then the Links

Suppose you have a daughter graduating from high school. She's seventeen and wants to know more about church-related colleges. Bang—a link, prepared by the college itself. She's immediately aware of church-related opportunities.

Suppose you are curious about the $1,000 gift you gave to UMCOR or Church World Service when Katrina devastated New Orleans. A click and you discover different categories: government money that went to UMCOR to develop a counseling/organizational infrastructure; money from the churches through a Bishop's Appeal to give direct aid to destitute families; money now requested to rebuild churches and parsonages.

Suppose you want to know more. Suppose you want to know more about the malaria epidemic in Africa. Or you read in *Time* magazine about former president Bill Clinton and Microsoft's Bill Gates focusing millions of dollars on malaria prevention and treatment, and cooperating with Bishop Machado and church structures in order to get relief and medical care into the villages. Would you like to learn about Nothing But Nets? Did you know that *Sports Illustrated* magazine, The National Basketball Association, and the United Nations Foundation are cooperating with your church to reduce malaria? Ten dollars will buy a net and save a life. Click on nothingbutnets.net or umc.org/nets.

Suppose your high school daughter reads about students who receive "Dollars for Scholars" to help with college expenses. Or your college son wants to serve people through Project Transformation or US 2 programs. They click on the link.

Who Does the Work?

But who is going to perform the labor? First of all, organizations want everyone to know about their thing. If you are president of a college, you would like every high school student in the world to know the dramatic details of your school. If you are head of a board of missions, you wish everyone who ever put a dollar in the collection plate could visit the medical clinic in Nairobi, the orphanage in Manila, or the school for girls in Calcutta. If you are the bishop of Indiana, you have a story to tell, but you are frustrated in trying to tell it. Imagine how eager you would be to prepare a link-story that folks could click on.

Carry it further. You read about a mission school, say, Lydia Patterson Institute in El Paso, Texas, and you are thrilled at the fabulous training they provide for kids from Juarez, Mexico. You decide to swipe your credit card and give $50. Done!

Did you know the computer can count the hits on your link? Imagine how excited the director of the orphanage in Manila would be if their link had 1,300 hits last month. Would they ever be motivated to keep their story fresh and dramatic!

So, the home church secretary or a volunteer has the easy job of keeping the daily local update. Now, the agencies and institutions, frustrated as a bull locked up in the barn in springtime, hungry to tell their stories, will knock themselves out to make fresh updates available on their link. (Many are now doing that, but only the most aggressive searchers are willing to ferret it out.)

The entire enterprise depends on a middleman. That's where the *Reporter* steps in. They latch on to Yahoo—making use of both their expertise and their worldwide news resources. They discover and spawn link sources from church organizations and institutions. They contact local churches and help develop their home pages. Congregational families are told by their local church how to, with a click, access their own church's home page. The cost to the family, nothing; to the institution or agency, nothing more than what they are now doing. Money needed by the *Reporter* to support the portal costs the local church only a few hundred dollars a year. The actual labor is shared by millions of folks like you and me all over the world, who click on once or twice a day and call it play. You can see it now at UMPortal.org.

And there is even more. Now available at www.BeADisciple.com, sponsored by the Institute for Discipleship at Southwestern College, are online workshops. You want to plan a mission trip to Haiti? Have a few members click on to an inexpensive workshop given by Volunteers in Mission (VIM) specialists. Without leaving their homes, members can, with a few clicks on their keyboards, learn details for conducting a successful trip. Would you like to study how to make DISCIPLE Bible study flourish and grow in your community? Take a three-week, online workshop (www.beadisciple.com).

Or perhaps you are planning an expanded vacation Bible school, or hoping for a new contemporary worship service. The Institute for Discipleship and the *United Methodist Reporter* are committed to giving the local church, clergy and laity, immediate access to the best thinking in the church today. Just as DISCIPLE brought top biblical scholars into homes and churches by way of video/DVD presentations, now we are moving to the Internet with expertise that heretofore has been too costly, too remote, too time-consuming for most people to utilize. It's here.

It's a new day in communications. The church of Jesus has a story to tell—all around the world. People have a hunger to know and to feel connected. It's part of "the tie that binds."

Chapter 11 / LET'S GO TO PRISON

Jesus said . . . I was in prison and you visited me.

(Matt. 25:36)

Darrell Hayden, retired Coast Guard officer, then a fabricated steel salesman, closed his Bible, put it on top of his DISCIPLE manual, looked at his friend, Darrell Sayles, and said, "DISCIPLE is powerful. We need to do something with it or God is going to get us."

The year was 1995. The two Darrells had almost finished the 34-week DISCIPLE Bible study and had become close friends. Sayles, a quiet, middle-aged accountant, gently replied, "Let's pray about this and see what God would have us do." The next week, out of the blue, he said, "Wouldn't it be nice if people in prison could experience DISCIPLE?"

"That's it!" said Hayden. "That's what we need to do. Let's do it!" Sayles meant it only as a suggestion, but Hayden jumped at the idea.

The next day, the two laymen met with the Reverend Mark Hicks, young associate pastor of Mount Pisgah United Methodist Church in Greensboro, North Carolina, to discuss their crazy idea. Expecting rebuttal, they found encouragement instead. Without thinking, Mark said, "Good idea. Go ahead and do it." Suddenly piety shifted to performance.

So they approached the chaplain of a nearby work camp prison, a heavy-set man, a former inmate, who scowled, "We don't have room in the schedule for a Bible study." Undaunted, the laymen went to another nearby prison, the Forsyth Correctional Center, a minimum security unit, and there they met with the Reverend Mike Lee, associate chaplain. Chaplain Lee took it to his boss, the chief chaplain, who shouted, "Another Bible study? Get rid of them!"

But Chaplain Lee sensed the sincerity and commitment of the two Darrells and offered them the only time slot available: 10:00 a.m. on Saturdays. The laymen swallowed deep because they worked full time during the week and hated like thunder to give up Saturday mornings. But they agreed. That was the price of getting into prison and fulfilling their vision.

In Kentucky, the Reverend Gale Wetzel, conference evangelist, drove fifty to one hundred miles each week to prisons. He led DISCIPLE groups at Northpoint Prison near Danville, the Green River Complex near Central City, and the Marion Adjustment Center near Lebanon. Whose idea was that?

Mary Catherine McSpadden, wife of guitar maker Steve and daughter-in-law of the Reverend Byron McSpadden, sat with her pastor, the Reverend Steve Johnson at First United Methodist Church, Mountain View, Arkansas. They had just concluded DISCIPLE: MAKING DISCIPLES THROUGH BIBLE STUDY, and she said, "We ought to take this experience into prison." So the next fall they led a group of women at nearby Calico Rock Prison. Where did they get that inspiration?

From the ground up, from the grassroots, without plan or direction, DISCIPLE started going to prison. Bruce Cook, prison chaplain, led groups in Georgia. So did the Reverend Diane Parish—she even began a camp for children of inmates. Nancy Jackson, Larry Schuster, and Brian Buffum, lay persons with backgrounds in Kairos and Emmaus, broke into Kansas by leading DISCIPLE at the Winfield Correctional Facility.

Joanne White, wife of a businessman in Alexandria, Louisiana, started leading DISCIPLE in a prison where some of the inmates couldn't read or write.

Back in Arkansas, unknown to me as their bishop, Neva Shewmaker, Mary Beth Weidman, and Pastor Mike Morey from Paragould First United Methodist Church led DISCIPLE at the nearby women's prison. In Ohio, Bill Harris, retired businessman working with Restorative Justice Ministries and Kairos, organized DISCIPLE in several Ohio prisons.

If you say Pennsylvania I think German, not Spanish. I conjure up Amish buggies and Quaker churches and great universities like Penn State and Temple, not high prison walls topped by barbed wire. But when the Reverend Dave Heckman was sent to a five-point charge in the mountains above Altoona, Pennsylvania, in 1999, assisted by associate pastor Stan Nixon, they began to study the nearby federal prison in Loretto, where the walls are high and the barbed wire is sharp. Stan, before entering the ministry, had worked for years as a federal corrections officer, so he knew the soul hunger of prison inmates. He also knew the complicated rules and procedures of Christian ministry in a federal penitentiary.

So, as the two men finished their first DISCIPLE group in their Glasgow United Methodist parish, they looked toward the imposing prison walls, Dave rolling his eyes, Stan rubbing his hands in anticipation. So began the first DISCIPLE I classes in the maximum security Loretto Federal Prison for inmates, one of whom spoke both English and Spanish.

Before long, Dave and Stan discovered that the bilingual inmate was taking the study back to his prison block and sharing it with his Spanish-speaking brothers. So, without money, organizational structure, or outside guidance, the Johnston Prison Ministry began. Money for Bibles and DISCIPLE manuals was raised from Sunday school classes and nearby churches; volunteers, including Dave Heckman's wife, Dorie, joined in. The Reverend David Stains, pastor and onetime missionary to Nicaragua and fluent in Spanish, came aboard, and Dorie brushed up on her high school Spanish. Two classes began that autumn in English and Spanish—and a class in the camp at Loretto—and, as Dorie exclaimed, "We were hooked!"

Soon, our "outside" volunteers discovered internal conflict between blacks and Hispanics in the prison. Fights broke out; the groups stayed separate. But when the study groups, aided by the chaplain, began worship experiences prior to study time, "Real miracles began to occur!" Dorie writes. "The two racial groups, who previously could not get along at all, now were praising the Lord together and praying for each other every week. The chaplain and the officers said they could see the effects throughout the prison. God was moving mightily in FCI/Loretto."

Other volunteers got excited, additional churches began to help with the finances. Soon the movement expanded into two state prisons, one county women's prison, and three youth facilities. Now the "Prison Outreach Ministry" became an official Advance Special of the Annual Conference. Stan Nixon left his pastoral work and became a full-time General Board of Global Ministries Missionary in Prison Ministry. DISCIPLE II, III, and IV were offered. (Spanish scholar the Reverend Stains translated DISCIPLE II, III, and IV manuals, and ran off copies on his church printer.)

You may be wondering about the Spanish-speaking inmates in a Pennsylvania prison. I wondered too. I learned that men and women in Latin America are recruited, bribed, sometimes threatened with their lives or the lives of their families to be carriers of drugs—often called "mules." They carry illicit drugs, sometimes in their stomachs, to the States and, if apprehended, end up in federal prison.

One afternoon in May 2004, I left the General Conference of The United Methodist Church meeting in Pittsburgh, Pennsylvania, and traveled by car to the ominous—and somewhat frightening (to me)—federal prison at Loretto. That evening I entered the prison, carefully provided credentials to the officers at the gate, and walked with the chaplain and DISCIPLE leaders to a roomful of inmates—black, white, and Hispanic men. I listened to moving testimonies in English and Spanish. I gave a brief talk of encouragement and then handed out fifty-nine DISCIPLE certificates. The head chaplain, a tough, no-fooling-around, in-charge lady, said the ministry had transformed the prison climate.

As I write this, Prison Outreach Ministry in Western Pennsylvania has forty-seven volunteers serving over 250 inmates in four federal, five state, and two county prisons; two youth detention centers; and one shelter. They now have, as current missionary director, the Reverend Randy Datsko, commissioned in 2004, helping at Federal Correction Institute, Loretto. They work with Prison Fellowship to provide mentors for inmates and to assist for one year in helping released inmates find housing, work, and a church home. An interesting sidelight: the federal prison put a two-year ban on all religious studies, then invited our Pennsylvania friends to come back with DISCIPLE because it was "a disciplined study that required participation (reading and studying) and accountability from the inmates."

Whose lives are being changed? Everyone's. Some volunteers have served for several years, saying their lives will never be the same. Others say they came in to the prison to "bring Christ" to the inmates but find they "take home more than they give." Churches are becoming more mission-minded, and when released inmates come to church, members gain new insight into Christian fellowship with persons who are "different."

Inmates have become leaders of new DISCIPLE groups in prison. Dorie writes, "One of our Spanish-speaking brothers being released is planning to lead a DISCIPLE study in his hometown in South America! Praise the Lord!"

My question is, where on God's green earth did this idea come from? I've attended all the meetings of DISCIPLE—from the first discussion in Nashville, through the consultation in Flower Mound, Texas. Julia and I wrote the manuals, consulted constantly with the United Methodist Publishing House. The word *prison* was never mentioned!

I have belonged to several general boards, sit on the Council of Bishops, attend General Conference. No one ever suggested taking DISCIPLE to prison. You would think we didn't own a Bible. I've been reading Matthew 25, preaching and listening to sermons on that passage all my life. When Jesus said, "I was hungry," we fed people all over the world. When he said, "I was naked," we established Goodwill Industries and gave clothes to the Salvation Army. He said, "I was sick and you visited me," and countless pastors and lay people are seen daily in the hospitals and care homes across the land. But I and most all the churches quit reading (and listening) when Jesus said, "I was in prison and you visited me" (Matt. 25:36).

The early Wesleyans were more faithful to the message. John and Charles Wesley and other members of the Holy Club at Oxford went to the awful, disease-ridden prisons of England. They washed wounds, smuggled in food for the starving, prayed for inmates facing execution. Later Wesley admonished his Methodist preachers to go to the prisons regularly, at first trying to save souls, later also working for prison reform.

I'm not forgetting good people across my lifetime: laymen who have taken Gideon Bibles to jails and prisons, priests and pastors who have given holy communion to inmates, prison chaplains who have offered their lives in prison ministries, and the Kairos movement—the ecumenical prison ministry that sprang from Cursillo and Emmaus. I'm not forgetting; I'm confessing, for myself and for churches that definitely have put the spotlight of their attention and the bulk of their energies elsewhere for a long time.

Prisons in America

But now, we're working up to these unusually difficult but profound ministries. And it's about time! For we face a crisis in America. Do you know how many inmates we have in jails and prisons in our fair land? Over two million men and women, boys and girls currently are incarcerated; over six million people are awaiting trial, out on bond, in jails, on work release, or on probation. One-fourth of all the prisoners *in the world* are in American jails.

Most states, like Kansas and Texas, are embroiled in legislative and budget controversy over where and how and with what money can they build more prisons. Some states, like North Carolina, have tried, unfortunately, selling their prisoners to "for profit" jails.

I'm not an expert, but whenever I talk to career prison chaplains or prison officials, I say, "Most of the prisoners or former inmates I've encountered have (a) come from broken homes, (b) are addicted to drugs and alcohol, or (c) have learning disabilities." They always nod their heads in agreement.

Some of our laws have backfired. A few years ago, Congress decided to crack down on big drug dealers, so they passed severe drug laws, including the mandatory minimum sentence: "Three strikes and you're out." Unfortunately, most of the truly big dealers are still operating, but kids on the street, soon addicted to cocaine or meth, get picked up, sentenced, imprisoned, and, still addicted, get in trouble as soon as they get out. Add to the fact that most inmates are released without jobs, with no job skills, without money, friends, or family and we have a 65 percent to 75 percent recidivism rate of inmates returning to prison.

Today I am visiting the Sedgwick, Kansas, County Jail, where a former inmate was arrested once again for possession of cocaine. While the state legislature debates a mandatory drug treatment program (a year under mandatory treatment), he faces—with no discretion from the judge—a fifty-nine–month sentence. Many judges are complaining that discretion has been torn from their judgments. Today, just as in Wesley's day, once we become deeply involved with prisoners, we become intensely interested in prison reform.

But our heartbeat, our passion must begin with, as Wesley said, the "saving of souls." DISCIPLE's goal—transformation not just information—has several built-in spiritual qualities. It is biblical without being judgmental. Unlike some pressure-packed Bible presentations that state you must believe thus and so, DISCIPLE encourages thoughtful discussion, even vigorous disagreement. Many inmates are at first defensive—something else is going to be laid on them—but they slowly begin to relax when they experience the nonjudgmental freedom.

When cooperative churches begin to wake up, like Gulliver rousing from a tied-down sleep, powerful things can happen. Isolated grassroots initiatives can be transformed into connected movements. Connectedness is marching into prison ministry.

Most of our prisons are state owned and operated. Rules and regulations, necessarily complicated and sometimes severe, vary from state to state, even from warden to warden. Over the past decade, men like Darrell Sayers and Darrell Hayden have knocked on the door of a nearby prison. Stan Nixon and the Heckmans slowly penetrated Pennsylvania's system, even launching DISCIPLE in state and federal penitentiaries. Once the integrity of the DISCIPLE leaders is established, once the long-term, nonmanipulative study produces fruit, local wardens turn receptive. They talk to other wardens. Chaplains share with chaplains of other prisons.

DISCIPLE Bible Outreach Ministries

In North Carolina, as the two Darrells told their story, DISCIPLE leaders in other churches began contacting their local prisons. Soon the bishops of North Carolina and Western North Carolina became interested. So did Annual Conference structures. They asked the Reverend Mark Hicks to supervise the movement; they provided money from churches. The DISCIPLE Bible Outreach Ministries was formed. Using trained DISCIPLE leaders, DBOM added "prison training" workshops, and they carefully obeyed all prison rules and guidelines. Soon the head of corrections for the state of North Carolina wrote a formal letter of recommendation affirming DISCIPLE's value in all state prisons. At last count, DISCIPLE ministries now reach seventy state prisons and involve over three hundred volunteer leaders. More than seven thousand inmates have participated. Annual Cross and Key banquets and annual training events maintain connection, stimulate enthusiasm, and support obedience to prison guidelines.

As other states gain momentum, always working from the ground up, the Reverend Mark Hicks and DBOM give counsel and support.* Here's how connectedness works. The Reverend Lu Ann Charlton of North Carolina traveled to New York state to train DISCIPLE leaders. One trainee was a prison chaplain. He was so moved he negotiated a meeting with Bishop Ernest Lyght, other church leaders, and prison officials. Then in December 2004, the Reverend Hicks led a DISCIPLE Prison Ministry Outreach training in White Plains, New York, with prison officials, prison chaplains (various denominations), clergy, and laity throughout New York in attendance. The New York prison system adopted DISCIPLE as "the primary Protestant prison curriculum for the entire system."

Other states tell similar stories. In Kansas, all doors were closed. When Larry Schuster and Nancy Jackson approached the friendly Baptist chaplain at the minimum-security Winfield Correctional Facility, they faced weeks of negotiation and prison orientation meetings. But once the door was opened, integrity and complete prison compliance established, other spiritual activities evolved. Voluntary worship services are held on Sunday. The prison opened its doors to the Interfaith Fellowship Institute (IFI), founded by Charles Colson and initiated in Texas. Brothers in Blue, an offshoot of Kairos, Cursillo, and Emmaus, was welcomed once a year.

Then, miracle of miracles, other prisons—tough, maximum-security prisons in Kansas—began to open up. Facilities in Hutchinson, Ellsworth, Larned, Lansing, and El Dorado, with high walls and barbed wire fences, now allow DISCIPLE and Brothers in Blue weekends. Layman Don Peter of Hutchinson helped gain entrance and recruited volunteer DISCIPLE facilitators. After his untimely death, layman James Wilson grabbed the reins. IFI has an entire wing devoted to volunteers. Church leaders are knocking on the door of the Leavenworth Federal Penitentiary. Still without funds or staff, informal conversations, e-mail, and training gatherings provide connectedness. In Houston, Texas, they call it Restorative Justice. A consortium of dedicated people of different denominations, along with some prison officials, have been working on prison reform, trying to help released inmates get jobs, holding ecumenical Kairos events, and working with IFI. Retired businessman Lou Aires and homemaker Vicki Schleimer give strong leadership. With Texas enthusiasm, they have raised money independently to support a former inmate, now a powerful preacher, to preach the gospel and tell his story.

What about you, the reader? Watch out, or you might get involved! A few years ago, Larry Schuster—that landscape gardener I've mentioned—invited me to join him and Brian Buffum, a General Electric engineer, to help guide a DISCIPLE group on Monday night at our local prison. I said I was "pretty busy," but they insisted. So I dutifully took the prison training (picture identification, no pocket knives, no sentimental writing of letters or making phone calls for the inmates).

My life will never be the same. The group of fourteen men was white, black, Hispanic, ages nineteen to fifty-two. Some had been in prison for a few months, some for twenty years. One man said he read with difficulty. It took him two or three hours a day to read his Bible assignment. But he smiled and said, "But I've got lots of time!"

One night, a man interrupted the discussion by asking rather abruptly, looking at Larry, Brian, and me, "Why are you guys here? You aren't getting paid, are you? You could be home with your families watching TV. Why are you here?" As best we could, we muttered out our faith in Christ, our love for them, our joy in studying the Scriptures together. And he responded, "This is the first time in my life anybody ever said they loved me."

One night, our youngest member, a Roman Catholic about nineteen, said he was getting out that week. Someone suggested we pray for him. The next thing I knew, he was on his knees, the group gathered around, hands on his head, praying that he would make it on the "outside." He has never returned. In fact, recidivism for DISCIPLE inmates ranges about 5 percent to 8 percent compared to the national rate of about 70 percent. (If it weren't for addiction to drugs, and our minimal after-care work, it would be even less.)

Connection causes other things to happen. Christian people in several states are helping with children of inmates. In Ohio, Georgia, and elsewhere, churches provide summer camps. Church women are often found taking children to see their mothers.

But whenever the words of Jesus, "I was in prison and you visited me," grab our minds and hearts, huge new challenges emerge. After scripture, the Holy Spirit, and Christian love have slain one dragon and brought an inmate to saving grace in Jesus our Lord, new monsters crawl out of the cave.

Juveniles

Consider juveniles: Tens of thousands of kids, nine- to sixteen-years-old, are in our detention centers and juvenile prisons. Many of them read with difficulty, often at the third- or fourth-grade level. The vast majority are from broken homes or no homes at all. Even Youth DISCIPLE, pitched for serious-minded high schoolers, is too difficult. Adult ministries like Kairos and Brothers in Blue fly above their heads.

When this juvenile dragon reared its head in North Carolina, DISCIPLE Bible Outreach Ministries (DBOM) with Mark Hicks and advisors who understand children and youth, prepared a study called RINGS of Fellowship. It is a youth Bible study program developed by DBOM of North Carolina, Inc., in partnership with the North Carolina Department of Juvenile Justice and Delinquency Prevention.

Why this program? They discovered that a high percentage of the boys and girls in North Carolina's Youth Development Centers re-offend and return to a Youth Development Center or to an adult prison within three years. Many of these children come from homes of crime, poverty, and abuse. RINGS was developed to help combat this tragic rate of return by offering at-risk youth the opportunity to grow spiritually and connect with a church following release.

So with a DISCIPLE manual on one side and juvenile advisors on the other, Mark Hicks prepared a six-month study—with the encouragement of state authorities. The study is divided into five sections with four lessons in each section—followed with an award ceremony after each four weeks! In the acronym RINGS, the R stands for Responsibility, the I for Individuality, the N for Neighbor, the G for God, and the S for Service.

The program was five years old in 2007, with more than fifty volunteers who have led groups. In August of 2007, with some aid from grant funds, a brand new RINGS DVD was produced. It provides skits and discussion questions in a fun format. It is hosted by Christan comedian the Reverend Andy Lambert. Now, what started in juvenile facilities is being used by children's groups in churches.

Folks in other states are taking a look. Some are experimenting. DBOM provides training and materials to all who inquire. Mark Hicks says that a recent spike in gang activity illustrates how much work needs to be done at the community level.

After Care

Realizing that many of the children and youth have no place to go upon release, DBOM initiated Bands of Support—an after-care component of the RINGS study. Churches and other faith communities provide mentoring and fellowship for youth returning home—youth who have requested support for their continued spiritual growth.

One of my DISCIPLE inmate friends, call him Max, had been in prison off and on for twenty years. By the fifth grade, homeless, he was on the streets, pimping and selling drugs. But at age forty-two he was assistant to the chaplain and leader of our DISCIPLE group.

When you get out of prison in Kansas, you are given $100. You have no car, no driver's license, no job, no friends, no place to live. You are on probation or in work-study. Max got a job as a fry cook in a steak house. A fire burned the steak house to the ground. Back on drugs, Max is back in prison.

Across the nation, churches are asking how they can provide friendship, Christian fellowship, halfway houses, job training, and guidance.

We are also asking why state governments would rather build more prisons and spend $25,000 to $30,000 a year per inmate, than establish drug treatment, job training, and drug-free halfway houses. (Can you believe Kansas is considering "private, for profit" prisons?) Something is wrong when, each year, hundreds of thousands of men and women who have paid their debt to society struggle helplessly in society, and then, in resignation more than rebellion, return to jail.

Local churches, once they get involved in prison ministry, once they start calling people by name—Herschel and Marie and Jose and Nathan—pray for them, and love them in Christ, begin to think "after care." North Carolina, Pennsylvania, Ohio, Oklahoma, and Kansas seem to be leading the way. A layman, Bill Harris, in Ohio, has helped local chuches open their hearts and doors to former inmates. His work is part of a comprehensive prison ministry. We have 34,000 United Methodist churches, many of them near a prison. What a ministry if the connection gets connected!

Stan L. Basler, former county attorney in Cherryvale, Kansas, watched as men and women went to prison battered and broken. In 1989, he heard the whispers of God and began seminary. Before he knew it, he was appointed associate to First United Methodist Church, Muskogee, Oklahoma, and his passion for prisoners burst forth like a spring garden. He assisted the chaplain, helped with prison worship services, organized an in-prison Christian Rural Overseas Program (CROP) walk, formed a Tuesday evening covenant group in a women's facility.

After four years, the bishop appointed this lawyer turned preacher as full-time director of Criminal Justice and Mercy Ministries. Stan Basler, aided of course by dedicated laity like Nancy Jackson and receptive pastors, has accomplished amazing prison ministries since 1994.

He transformed the Penn Avenue United Methodist Church in Oklahoma City into a "redemption church" with Sunday afternoon fellowship and worship for inmates and their families, a Thursday evening study, and worship groups.

He formed these Redemption Churches (inmates and their families) in existing churches in Tulsa, Lawton, and Ardmore, all in Oklahoma.

He developed "New Day" youth camps—ages 8-11 and 12-14—for children of the incarcerated.

Like all who work with prison inmates, Stan Basler knew, even after ministries like Kairos, DISCIPLE Bible study, covenant groups, and communal worship, crisis time crashes down when an inmate is released.

Without money or staff, Basler garnered funds to buy Exodus Houses in Tulsa and Oklahoma City. Totally separate from prison authorities, staffed by former inmates, the houses gave a place to live, help with jobs, and Christian fellowship to those men and women ready for a fresh start in a Christian environment.

Now, would you believe, they've even begun a charter school, the John Wesley Charter School, for juvenile offenders and troubled children in Oklahoma City. They are receiving full cooperation from juvenile authorities.

Now they've asked Stan to teach restorative justice at the Oklahoma City University School of Law—with a television connection to Saint Paul Seminary in Kansas City, Missouri. Where did the money come from? From folks like you and me. How did all this happen? From the grass roots, although now, in Oklahoma, the conference has institutionalized the work and is beginning to tell the rest of the world all about it. The work began with a passionate lawyer/preacher! Whose idea? Stan Basler says Jesus (Matt. 25:39) and Paul (1 Cor. 12).

Can you believe this? After a time of worship services and various ministries in the Iowa Correctional Institution for Women at Mitchellville, Iowa, the United Methodists formed a "duly constituted" congregation and Bishop Gregory Palmer appointed the Reverend Arnette Pint as pastor. She holds regular weekly services on Thursday evenings and works half time counseling with the women inmates and half time interpreting prison ministries in churches throughout Iowa. Partner churches send members to visit and worship with the women. The congregation is called "Women at the Well," and the partner churches also help with the finances. What a dramatic step in prison ministries!

Prison Reform

The early Wesleyans walked to prisons, like soldiers on duty, to save souls. Some prisoners were converted on the way to the gallows. But quickly those concerned Christians saw vast injustices in the system. Men were executed for stealing a loaf of bread. Widows were left destitute. Orphans ran homeless in the streets. The prisons were filthy, disease-ridden.

So today, Christians involved in prison ministries—from Charles Colson and IFI, to Catholic priests, and volunteers with Kairos, DISCIPLE, and Brothers in Blue—all are asking restorative justice questions:

a) Why a mandatory minimum sentence law that destroys the judges' discretion? "Three strikes and you're out" can imprison an alcoholic or drug addict forever.

b) Why so little attention to job skills and drug rehabilitation? We are asking why state governments would rather build more prisons and spend $25,000 to $30,000 a year per inmate, than establish drug treatment, job training, and drug-free halfway houses.

c) Why not, as Charles Colson argues, allow more recompense rather than punishment in nonviolent crime? Let the offender pay for the stolen groceries or clothes.

d) Why so little attention to after care?

What an opportunity for the church! We have churches near every prison in the land. They say we have more United Methodist churches in the United States than post offices. We will be especially effective if we know the former inmates by name, having shared the love of Christ with them while they were incarcerated. Some inmates have special permission to attend Sunday worship. Volunteers with DISCIPLE groups can invite those inmates to their congregations following release. Special Sunday school classes and small study groups are effective. First United Methodist Church, Wichita, Kansas, has formed a Sunday school class for men at the nearby work-release facility. First United Methodist Church, Winfield, Kansas, with prison permission, sends a layman in the church van to the Winfield minimum security prison to bring three or four inmates to Sunday school and worship. Some churches help provide housing or assist former inmates in finding a job. But friendship is the most vital ingredient. We're not talking about "schmaltz"—soft, naïve sentimentality. (Don Smarts is an old pro—the longtime president of Bill Glass Ministries. Read his hard-nosed, caring, Christ-centered book, *Keeping Ex-Offenders Free!*) No, we're pleading for church people to convert, study and pray with, aid where able, accept into fellowship with a tough, warm, Christ-centered love men and women who have made mistakes and want redemption.

I've stressed how prison ministries have sprung up like wildflowers with only God's sunshine and rain to bless them. A handful of laity going to a nearby prison, a zealot preacher formulating a Brothers in Blue or Kairos gathering, a group of churches operating a halfway house—all are ministries that are emerging locally.

But now, the higher-ups are taking notice. Some bishops are giving powerful support. General boards and agencies are looking for ways to pour organizational gasoline on the fire. Beginning in 2005, the General Board of Higher Education and Ministry of the United Methodist Church, which supervises United Methodist prison chaplains, launched cooperative studies of prison ministries. They are bringing together U.M. seminaries, U.M.-endorsed prison chaplains, and U.M. congregational-based prison ministries. Their goals are to rediscover the Wesleyan heritage of going to the prisons and to energize a comprehensive criminal justice initiative. Leaders of this movement include Dr. James Shopshire of Wesley Theological Seminary; Chaplain Richmond Stoglin of Dallas, Texas; Mark Hicks of DISCIPLE Bible Outreach Ministries; Betsey Heavner of the General Board of Discipleship; Dallas Terrell of ITC-(Interdenominational Theological Center) in Atlanta; and Pat Barrett and Saul Epanio of the General Board of Higher Education and Ministry.

In September 2005 the first Criminal Justice Summit of the United Methodist Church took place in Atlanta with over one hundred church leaders in attendance. During this event Otis Hardy, a former inmate whose life was transformed through the DISCIPLE prison ministry in North Carolina, was the keynote speaker. This summit was only the first step in this new initiative. With help from the General Board of Discipleship, a new interactive prison ministry website has been created and the prison ministry guidebook is being updated. Future plans include the publication of a new seminary text on prison ministry and the establishment of a yearly, two-week criminal justice academy.

But don't wait for the organization to get organized. Don't be like the fellow waiting for the city to tell him to mow his lawn. Take a couple of men or women, a handful of DISCIPLE manuals, and some Bibles, and go see your nearby prison chaplain. In the words of Nike, "Just do it!"

> Remember those who are in prison,
> as though you were in prison with them. (Heb 13:3)

*Disciple Bible Outreach
P.O. Box 4158, Archdale, NC 27263
disciple@nccumc.org

Postlude / **Just Do It**

Not everyone who says to me, "Lord, Lord," will enter
the kingdom of heaven,
but only the one who does the will of my Father in heaven.

(Matt. 7:21)

Have you noticed? Most of the exciting spiritual renewal events come from the bottom up. Few innovative enterprises come from the top down—from general boards or general conferences or councils of bishops. Like a Kansas winter wheat field, some seed is planted by a farmer and in late fall it sprouts, covering the field in green. But in the spring, it explodes, bursting into golden grain in June. So with church renewal.

Whose idea was the Ashram movement where I received the Holy Spirit? Just a wandering evangelist named E. Stanley Jones. Where did VIM (Volunteers in Mission) come from? The church leaders crushed Bob Kochtitzky of Mississippi when he tried to initiate LAOS (Laymen's Overseas Service) in the 1960s. They said lay people weren't properly trained, adequately insured. But here and there mission groups began; and now thousands of Christians organized in local churches and encouraged by church leaders, VIM workers, and other volunteers labor for Christ around the globe. You couldn't stop this movement with a bulldozer!

Whose idea was it to take DISCIPLE Bible study into the prisons? Ask Larry Schuster or Brian Buffum or Nancy Jackson in Kansas. Ask Mark Hicks in North Carolina or Stan Nixon and Dave and Debbie Heckman in Pennsylvania. They'll say it was God's idea. They had no money, no authority, no guidance. They believed, with God's help, in the Nike slogan, "Just do it."

Why did St. Luke's United Methodist Church in Oklahoma City go to the Presbyterians in Chicago and a United Methodist church in Fort Worth and turn their Sunday school upside down? Because they were dying. A lady named Charlotte Teel and a preacher named Robert Long decided to reach kids for Jesus, using modern learning techniques.

Whose idea was it for St. Luke's United Methodist Church, Houston, Texas, to start a "school after school"? I've never read a church article or attended any high-powered meeting advocating such a radical move. It came from the ground up.

When we first suggested a serious adult Bible study, scholarly videos, daily personal readings, and group discussion, church leaders smiled and said, "Don't call us, we'll call you. Americans are too busy and most people aren't interested in reading the Bible." So, sometime later, with the help of the publishing house, the movement began—a *Disciple* movement that today reaches around the world, has penetrated thirty denominations, and includes over two million participants.

My point? Who is going to start a new adult class in your church? Who is going to form a local "school after school" program, perhaps in cooperation with other denominations? Who is going to relate to a missionary in the field or a clinic or school in a distant land? Who is going to survey your town or neighborhood, crossing racial and cultural lines, and design a strategy for reaching new people? Who will preach a sermon inviting conversion? Or hold a healing service? Or offer experience of the Holy Spirit through surrender and the laying on of hands? Who will give a month teaching in rotation? Or five years working with youth? Who will lead a work team to Louisiana?

The answer is, "You, if it's going to happen." Others may notice what you're doing. Even top brass may tell others about your work. (They may also mention the conflict it caused, the criticism it spawned.)

But remember, Pentecost happened when a few hundred people got together and prayed in Jerusalem. Peter dreamed about eating with Cornelius. Paul heard the angel and decided to go to Greece. Martin Luther strolled the streets listening to the vernacular before translating scriptures into German. John Wesley walked with prisoners headed to the gallows, praying and reading scripture. Whose ideas were these?

Inspiration

Where does inspiration come from? Jesus promised, "Where two or three are gathered in my name, I am there among them" (Matt. 18:20). He also promised the Holy Spirit to the open and receptive. Christian innovators have always testified that the Holy Spirit—the quiet spirit of Jesus speaking in their hearts and minds—was the genesis, the inspiration for new, innovative Christian action.

The Challenge

So, this book has been a plea for those of us who claim his name to tackle a corrupt, secular, scripturally ignorant, lonely world with fresh enthusiasm. Like innovators in the computer world, let's be entrepreneurs for Jesus. Like Wal-Mart going to China, let's study cultures and make the gospel relevant.

In a world of communication, let us remember our Lord's admonition, "Go ... make disciples ... teaching them to obey everything that I have commanded you. And remember, I am with you always, to the end of the age" (Matt. 28:19-20)

See, we don't even have to do it alone. He will be with us.

> Blest be the tie that binds
> Our hearts in Christian love.
> The fellowship of kindred minds
> Is like to that above.

Study Guide

Chapter 1: Back to Square One

Summary

This chapter is a call to action for all Christians to return to their spiritual beginnings, including dependence upon the Holy Spirit, prayer, fellowship, building personal character, and being faithful to the theology of John Wesley.

Discussion Questions

Share your interest in reading this book and discussing the issues it addresses.

Discuss the reasons it is imperative for the church to return to its beginnings.

Has the church forgotten how to help people get started in faith? Give your opinion and an example.

Do you agree with the author's statement that too many sermons are aimed at the faithful and too few at the seeker? Explain your answer.

Discuss John Wesley's three forms of grace and how grace is relevant today.

How does controversy over interpretation of the Bible harm the church?

Discuss where the church remains faithful to the Wesleyan tradition and, in your opinion, where it has strayed.

Do you think there is less emphasis today on the Holy Spirit? If so, why?

Discuss how Robert Schnase created an open, disciple-making congregation.

Share your own opinion as to the priorities facing the church today.

Activities

As a group: Compile a report card for the church today. Divide into two groups. One group will create a list of what is right with the church today. The second group will list the shortcomings. Together, discuss your lists, then grade the church on what you identify as major priorities, including evangelism, worship, hospitality, Bible study, and so on.

As a group: Use your Bible to compare and contrast the challenges facing the early church with the challenges facing the church today.

Prayer

Dear God, thank you for opening our eyes to the problems facing the church today. Help us to be part of your solution to a world that needs Jesus. Amen.

Chapter 2: A Famine in the Land

Summary

This chapter provides evidence of the drought of spiritual knowledge and thirst for God's Word today. It shows how the world is drowning in sex, drugs, alcohol, dishonesty, crime, and human suffering.

Discussion Questions

Share how your spiritual upbringing was different from that of many of today's young people.

List some of the basics all youth should know about scripture.

Discuss the reasons the Bible is not being read and studied today.

How does a person become spiritually passionate?

List some reasons you believe Sunday school has dropped down on the list of people's priorities. Is it still a priority for most churches?

Discuss why people are falling down, never to get up. How and why are the words of Amos coming true?

Who is to blame for the problems faced by young people today?

How do you begin to identify and educate the spiritually illiterate?

Discuss the implications of lack of spiritual knowledge in America.

How is the church reacting to the famine in our land? What is and is not being done? What more needs to be done?

Activities

As a group: Create a group list of symptoms of a person who is spiritually starving. Discuss how you know when someone is spiritually sick.

As a group: Ask each group member to write down ten benefits of reading the Bible on a daily basis. Share your results and discuss how the Bible gives you spiritual nourishment.

Prayer

Dear God, thank you for this discussion of the spiritual thirst that is sweeping our land. Help us keep up our spiritual nourishment through prayer and Bible reading as we strive to do your will. Amen.

Chapter 3: Look at All the Lonely People

Summary

This chapter examines why so many people are so lonely and how the church can minister to their disconnectedness through small groups and Christian fellowship.

Discussion Questions

Share a time that you felt lonely. What feelings were triggered? How did you cope?

Discuss the many different ways that people cope with loneliness. Name some good and bad strategies for battling loneliness.

List some of the causes and reasons that many people often feel disconnected.

How and why are many people alienated from the church? Why does the church often scare people?

List some of the signs or symptoms of a disconnected person.

What role does the explosion of electronic entertainment and technology play in causing many of today's problems?

Discuss the two ways successful churches break down and attack disconnectedness.

Share the reason and wisdom behind the Wesley Class Meeting.

Discuss the issues, observations, and suggestions raised by authors Putnam and Feldstein.

Why is the small group experience helpful for getting people to connect and to grow spiritually?

Activities

As a group: Give each member a sheet of paper and ask them to create a personal invitation for their friend John or Jane Doe to attend church with them. Include how the church has blessed you and how it can bless them. Share your ideas about what people need to hear who do not have a church home.

As a group: Pair up and practice inviting a person to church and talking a bit about your faith. Switch roles so each person gets to be talker and listener. Share how your experience went with the whole group.

Prayer

Dear God, thank you for providing all we need to help those who are lonely and disconnected. Open our eyes to see those in need. Help us respond in love and compassion. Amen.

Chapter 4: Adults

Summary

This chapter looks at the needs of the church in order to meet the spiritual hunger of adults. It examines different ways of reaching adults and ministering to them.

Discussion Questions

Discuss what surveys show about churches today.

How can experts help churches have successful starts?

Explain why and how some churches are spiritually schizophrenic.

Discuss the challenges faced by churches in response to changed neighborhoods.

Name some of the myths and realities connected to adult Sunday school classes.

What strategies work for launching an adult class?

List and discuss ways to minister to those who are single.

Why can mission be an important tool for bringing people into the church?

What ideas work for identifying and using gifts and graces?

Give a summary of the needs and requirements of today's church.

Activities

As a group: If you were to survey people living near your church, what questions would you ask? Create a group list of survey questions and discuss them.

As a group: Brainstorm some ideas for mission that would appeal to both church members and non-church members. Identify your top three mission ideas.

Prayer

Dear God, thank you for all the opportunities that are available to minister in your name. Help equip us and your church to seek the spiritually hungry and feed them with the bread of life. Amen.

Chapter 5: Bigger Is Smaller

Summary

This chapter studies the traits of growing churches and looks at the small things that make a difference.

Discussion Questions

Discuss what surveys show about "spiritual interest" in America today.

What strategies did Rick Warren use to launch his church?

Explain why, when it comes to fellowship, smaller is better.

Discuss the two mistakes that DISCIPLE churches often make.

What was John Wesley's formula for church growth?

If you study growing churches, what do they have in common?

List and discuss the responsibilities of people who join a church.

Why does having an intimate church family keep members from backsliding?

What is needed in order for declining churches to turn around and grow?

Name and discuss the strategies for reaching new people that seem to work best. Give a summary of what works.

Activities

As a group: What should be expected of a church member? As a group, create a list of "rules" and expectations for church members. Talk about the need for rules and whether enforcement is practical.

As a group: Brainstorm simple acts and actions members can take to help their church grow.

Prayer

Dear God, thank you for showing us the importance of small and intimate church ministries. Guide our thoughts and actions so we can become part of the solution to problems within the church. Amen.

Chapter 6: Youth

Summary

This chapter examines the traits and spiritual needs of youth and looks at ways to minister to them.

Discussion Questions

Discuss what is known about teenagers today.

What pressures do teens face?

Why are college students suspicious? How can this be overcome? What do college students respond to?

Discuss what young people want and need within the church.

Why do you think loneliness is a problem for today's youth?

Why do young people want to be leaders? What do they have to offer the church?

Discuss the cultural gap in worship. What do you think can be done about it?

Give a summary of the elements of informal college student worship services.

How does youth worship music differ from music in traditional churches?

Give an overview of how and why the church needs to minister to youth.

Activities

As a group: Brainstorm ideas for serving as youth mentors.

As a group: Create a list of spiritual topics of special interest to youth. What could be done with your list?

Prayer

Dear God, thank you for the energy and enthusiasm youth bring to the church. Open our eyes so we can see opportunities to minister to them and meet their spiritual and emotional needs. Amen.

Chapter 7: Children

Summary

This chapter looks at the spiritual needs of children and ways to minister to them.

Discussion Questions

Discuss the origins of Sunday school and use of the Bible by the Wesleyan denominations.

Why are attendance and membership declining at many churches?

What new strategies are being used to reach children?

Discuss the advantages of the rotational Sunday school model.

What is LIVE B.I.G. and why is this experience so successful?

Discuss the benefits of Wednesday night programming at church.

Compare your childhood to the childhood of children today.

Discuss the author's idea for after school and identify the needs that it meets.

What basics of faith do all children need to know?

Share a new insight about ministry to children that you learned from this lesson.

Activities

As a group: Take an inventory of the resources available for children's ministry at your church. Is anything lacking? How can this ministry be improved?

As a group: Brainstorm other innovative ways to minister to children. Create a list of suggestions.

Prayer

Dear God, thank you for the privilege of introducing children to Jesus. Help us to be more effective in ministering to children and meeting their spiritual needs. Amen.

Chapter 8: Worship

Summary

This chapter looks at the different elements and methods of church worship. It offers a reminder of the importance of excellence and being creative to meet the needs of worshippers.

Discussion Questions

Share your favorite part of the worship service.

If you were to make one change to the worship service, what would it be and why?

Discuss the reasons behind the worship revolution.

How has the use of music and hymns been changed to enhance worship?

Discuss the audience for and appeal of a contemporary worship service.

How has the physical nature and layout of the sanctuary changed to accommodate new styles of worship?

When people come to Sunday worship, what type of worship experience do they want? What are their expectations?

Discuss the new ways the gospel message is being communicated during worship.

Why is thematic unity important? How is this unity created?

Name some of the keys to excellence in worship.

Activities

As a group: Create a list of words that describe the ideal worship experience.

As a group: Ask each member to use their creativity and drawing skills to create an illustration that portrays an image of worship. Compare the many different images created.

Prayer

Dear God, thank you for the freedom to worship you in any way we choose and at any church we choose. Help us make worship more meaningful for ourselves and others. Amen.

Chapter 9: Conflict in the Church

Summary

This chapter explores conflicts in the church and why homosexuality has divided many people and churches.

Discussion Questions

Share how you personally try to deal with conflict.

Discuss some of the conflicts in the early church. Name some of the more recent conflicts.

Do you think denominationalism helps or hinders the Christian faith? Explain.

Why is homosexuality a difficult subject for so many people? Why do people feel so strongly about this issue?

Why does the conflict over homosexuality continue in the church and why can't it be resolved? Is any progress being made? Why?

Do you agree or disagree with the author's views on this subject? Explain.

Discuss how the Bible can be used and misused to justify beliefs.

Why do many people believe that homosexuality is not a choice?

How have church conflicts like this been resolved in the past?

How should the church deal with this issue and other controversial issues?

Activities

As a group: Create a generic list of creative ways to resolve a conflict.

As a group: Search the Bible for justifications for slavery, then discuss how the passages were taken out of context. How are the topics of homosexuality and slavery similar? How are they dissimilar?

Prayer

Dear God, thank you for your diverse creation of all people. Each person is unique and loved by you. Help us settle our conflicts and focus on you and what really matters. Amen.

Chapter 10: Communication

Summary

This chapter examines the revolution in communication methods and looks at how new technology can be applied to reaching others for Christ.

Discussion Questions

List some of the many ways and methods that people use to communicate today.

Discuss why people often have no idea what is happening within their church or in world ministry.

How and why is the method of congregational church news changing?

Share a time you felt uninformed about something within your church.

Why are links on Internet websites so valuable for spreading information?

How could the Internet be used to raise funds for church ministry?

What opportunities are missed when the church fails to communicate effectively?

Discuss ways that lay people can get involved in this communication revolution.

Identify some ways new technology can be used to help people grow spiritually.

What new insights and ideas did you gain from this reading and discussion?

Activities

As a group: Conduct an inventory of the tools and resources your church has to communicate with members. What could be added to enhance communication within your church?

As a group: Brainstorm how many ways there are to promote summer vacation Bible school at your church. Rank the most innovative ideas suggested.

Prayer

Dear God, thank you for giving us new ways to spread the gospel of Jesus Christ. Help us embrace new ways of communicating with others so we can be both united and informed Christians. Amen.

Chapter 11: Let's Go to Prison

Summary

This chapter looks at the challenges and opportunities of ministering to those in America's prisons.

Discussion Questions

What impresses you most about prison ministry today?

Name some of the benefits of offering a prison ministry.

Discuss how language barriers can and are being overcome.

How do many stories in this chapter illustrate how God works in mysterious ways?

Discuss the variety of roles open to volunteers in prison ministry.

When it comes to prison reform, what works and what is not working?

What results concerning DISCIPLE ministry impressed you and why?

Discuss some of the costs of ministering to those in prison.

How can prayer be used to help and minister to prisoners?

What new insights about prisons and ministry opportunities did you receive from reading this chapter and discussing it?

Activities

As a group: Have a graduation celebration to mark the completion of this small group study.

As a group: Brainstorm ways to minister to those in prison in your spare time.

Prayer

Dear God, thank you for challenging us to minister to those in prison. Help us put a high value on all human life. Thank you for our time together and all the sharing that has taken place. Be with us as we go our separate ways. Amen.